Clean and Organize Your Home Bundle

2 Books in 1:

The Ultimate Room by Room Guide to Tidy Up Your House Through Minimalist Living and Deep Clean All Your Rooms

By

Grace Burke

While every precaution has been taken in the preparation of this book, the publisher assumes no responsibility for errors or omissions, or for damages resulting from the use of the information contained herein.

This book is for entertainment and informational purposes only. The views expressed are those of the author alone and should not be taken as expert instruction or commands. The reader is responsible for his or her own actions. Neither the author nor the publisher assumes any responsibility or liability whatsoever on behalf of the purchaser or reader of these materials. The reader is responsible for their own use of any products or methods mentioned in this publication.

This book includes information about products and equipment offered by third parties. As such, the author does not assume responsibility or liability for any third party products or opinions. Third party product manufacturers have not sanctioned this book, nor does the author receive any compensation from said manufacturers for sharing information regarding their products.

CLEAN AND ORGANIZE YOUR HOME BUNDLE
First edition. January 12, 2020
Copyright © 2019 Grace Burke.

Print ISBN: 978-1-64786-227-5

Table of Contents

Introduction 6
Chapter 1. Letting Go 11
Chapter 2. Minimalist Shopping 18
Chapter 3. Living Room 30
Chapter 4. Bedrooms 38
Chapter 5. Laundry Room 46
Chapter 6. Kitchen and Dining 55
Chapter 7. Minimalist Home Office 68
Chapter 8. Minimalist Storage 79
Chapter 9. Minimalist Exterior 88
Conclusion 100
Introduction 104
Chapter 1: The Purpose of a Clean Home 107
Chapter 2: The Best Supplies For Every Surface 113
Chapter 3: DIY Cleaning Mixes 129
Chapter 4: Decluttering Steps You Can't Skip 137
Chapter 5: Kitchen 143
Chapter 6: Living Areas 151
Chapter 7: Bedrooms 159
Chapter 8: Bathrooms 164
Chapter 9: Floors 172

Chapter 10: Additional Areas 179

Chapter 11: 7 Day Cleaning Plan 186

Chapter 12: Maintenance & Monthly Habits 201

Conclusion 211

Bibliography 215

Minimalist Home Secrets

The Ultimate Guide to Declutter and Organize Your Home
Through Minimalist Living

By

Grace Burke

Introduction

I inherited my 3,000 square foot clutter-filled home from my mother when she passed away. When some children inherit their parents' homes with their contents, they call in a service to catalogue and tag items to sell. They talk to a real estate agent about listing the house. They talk through division of profits with other heirs. Unfortunately, there was none of that when I found out the house was mine. My mother's house was thoughtfully built as a retreat for immediate family and to accommodate family members during important holidays. It wasn't supposed to be near a major metropolitan area and it wasn't meant to be sold off to provide a nest egg to anyone in my family. The house contained the clutter of countless possessions of my mother and past generations. It contained pieces I remember growing up with and ones more recently salvaged and made new again. It wasn't going to be a cut and dry inheritance. It was going to be so much more.

Soon after receiving the keys, I found myself standing in the entrance feeling both emotional and overwhelmed. Each item was brought here by my mother's hand, but altogether, the clutter was too much. Too much to allow myself and the rest of the family peace when staying here. Too much to wrangle in a weekend of furiously packing boxes. This house needed more than the conventional walk-through and gathering of favorite pieces before selling off the rest. It needed a heavy dose of minimalism.

It was fairly easy deciding to keep the house rather than sell it. It maintains its own charm sitting nestled in the mountains with trees lined around it. Winter nights deliver such a remarkable stillness you feel as though you're the only being left on Earth. When the wind whips through the lush trees on a summer afternoon, you feel revitalized. The decision to keep the house was easy, but accepting the task of applying minimalist principles was a bit daunting. There were many items in the home I knew could never leave. There were other items, however, that still held important meaning in the family, but did not serve a purpose anymore. Unfortunately, that distinction was lost when I found everything piled together and covered in a layer of dust. In its current state, there was no way to honor the special pieces and separate them from curbside finds. Accepting that fact, I found applying minimalist principles to my mother's house was the best way to bestow honor on family heirlooms. It would allow me to bring focus to the pieces that represented us best and to the items that serve us well.

Honoring my family's pieces was important, but I wasn't looking to build a museum. I wanted the house to fulfill its original purpose as a gathering place for family. I wanted to see twenty or so family members seated around the dining table originally used to feed workers on my great-grandmother's farm. I desired each of the bedrooms perfectly appointed for peaceful rest. I envisioned the grand living room hosting family for game night while a fire in the hearth kept us warm. The goal I envisioned would bring the serenity and respite one expects from a vacation home. The practice of minimalism helped me achieve my goal and this book is here to help you achieve your own.

I found my family especially supportive of my goal. They, too, could see how the clutter and extraneous items distracted from the beauty of the home. The prospect of retreating to the home on holidays and finding comfortable uncluttered surroundings was irresistible to them. It was time to get started. Items not suitable for hosting family were donated to charity or sold. Some items called out to be given to family and friends as reminders of their relationship with my mother. For all the physical and financial gain, this particular emotional gain stands out as a highlight. I even found new homes for items I had moved in with, but ended up being duplicates. When finding homes for these duplicates, I considered their usefulness for the intended recipient. I had found a new balance in my relationship with objects in my home and wanted to make sure I didn't tip the balance of someone else's home with my gift.

I knew my experience practicing minimalism in my new-to-me home contained many lessons others would find helpful. I wrote this book with those lessons in mind. Each chapter can help you methodically transform your home into a place of peace, gratification, and purposeful living. For our purposes, "Minimalism" simply means movement toward simplicity and away from consumerism. The push and pull actions inside the definition lead to balance. Balance that can fuel a more fulfilled life. Even if you aren't a devotee to modern minimalism, this book contains lessons to benefit all homeowners.

You may have tried a minimalist approach before and found it too daunting. Or perhaps you're like me and received an inheritance of clutter. It may be your first foray into the practice of minimalism. Wherever you begin, the words on these pages will support you in letting go of unnecessary items. You'll learn how to part with the many extraneous heirlooms passed down from generations before you. You will learn the best strategies to avoid overspending and discover actionable steps to open up every room in your home.

Minimalism is not synonymous with perfection. Modern minimalist living is a practice of awareness and intention regarding your belongings, time, and energy. By practicing minimalism, it becomes the lens through which we see the world and ourselves. It creates alignment with the objects in our lives and our purpose. When I stand in my mother's house now, I see only the best representations of her and our family. Before, my relationship with the objects in the house and the purpose I envisioned was out of alignment. Frustration and stress levels both ran high.

As I moved further along in my practice, I found physical benefits in addition to emotional and financial ones. I'm amazed at how quickly I can clean my house now that extraneous furniture and clutter has moved on. I never worry about unexpected guests or last-minute dinners with friends because my house stays cleaner for longer. The compliments I receive on the new layout of furniture and the exhibition of prized family heirlooms motivates me to continue this practice. The physical calmness I gain from more clear space on the walls and floors is immeasurable.

The changes in my emotional well-being as a result of decluttering are not unique. A 2009 UCLA study "No Place Like Home" linked the association of words like "clutter" and "unfinished" with one's home as indicative of that person's stress level. The frequency of word usage was shown to have a direct effect on the release of the stress hormone cortisol. The way we see our home and our objects really does correlate with our mood, and thus our emotional well-being.

A different study conducted by psychologist and researcher NiCole R. Keith, Ph.D. at Indiana University found that tidier homes increased an individiual's level of physical activity, thereby reducing the risk for cardiovascular disease. This conclusion took the study by surprise as it looked at the many factors that impact a person's level of physical activity. A positive attitude about the space we inhabit can affect our physical health just as it affects our emotional health.

You chose this book because you're tired of tripping over clutter at every turn. You're finished with overpacked closets that provide nothing in the way of organization or functionality. You've taken multitudes of items to local charities only to see more items creep in to your home. You're ready to walk into your home and feel peace, not a sense of dread from mountains of clutter. You're searching for the contentment of a well-organized home. This book is here to guide you on your journey to the serenity you seek.

There's never been a better time to get started as the waves of consumerism grow larger than ever. We're constantly receiving advertisements to purchase more items, to solve our problems with one more piece of clutter. It's time to turn away from the weight of the consumerist life and move towards a sense of harmony that comes from minimalism. This book contains everything you need to find balance in your relationship with the pieces in your home.

I'm excited for you to begin this journey and experience revitalization, one room at a time.

Chapter 1. Letting Go

Essential Mental Shifts You Need

Each chapter in this book contains vital information to help you practice modern minimalism successfully. In this first chapter, the most important power mindsets are laid out for you to absorb and manifest at the very start of your journey. In order to adjust the objects in your home, you must first adjust your mindset toward them. Different objects require different lines of thinking and in this chapter you'll find successful strategies to part with anything. I had many family heirlooms in my home, but I also had items like a faded favorite dress that still held a place in my heart. Knowing how to interact with each object made my 3,000 square foot project bearable. It will help make yours bearable, as well.

Power Mindset 1 - "Always be Thankful"

Gratitude is one of the strongest emotions and one of the most transformative. We experience gratitude as an instant emotion upon receiving a gift or other positive gesture. We can also practice it, which is encouraged for those seeking more balance in their life. Practicing gratitude with the objects in our homes helps bring balance between the objects and your purpose. It is the first power mindset because it underlies the entire practice of modern minimalism. Gratitude for our homes and their contents is what allows us to move forward in the practice.

To practice this mindset, take a step outside of the room you're about to begin organizing. Before entering, deeply inhale and exhale for 10 breaths. I want you to calm your heart as well as your thoughts. Step through the entrance to the room and stand in the middle. Look at all of the objects and furniture as you slowly turn about the room. Think of the many ways in which these items found their way into your home. The friends and family who gifted you with an item. The promotion at work that led you to purchase an item as celebration. The worn out items that have given you all their use. Be thankful for their contributions to your space and your life.

Once you have done that, begin with one item at a time. Hold it, remember its origin, and be thankful for its service to you. Even if you don't intend to get rid of an item, you want to renew your gratitude for it. By giving it recognition, you're bestowing positivity that will collect with the positivity from other items in your home. This helps support the peace and calm you seek from organizing your home.

We come by the objects in our homes in various ways: inheritance, gifts, our own selection and purchase. The power mindset, "Always Be Thankful," can be used for any object, but is especially powerful when applied to objects given to us. We often find it difficult to get rid of something that was a gift. Especially if we see the giver on a regular basis. But it is not possible to keep every gift ever given to us. Even though items are no longer in your physical possession, you remain grateful for having received them. The emotion of gratitude lasts far beyond the physical object.

Power Mindset 2 - "I'll Get Something Better"

How many times have you rifled through your medicine cabinet or clothes dresser and found items that you bought because they were needed at the time? Maybe it's a $1 comb picked up in a Chicago drugstore when the wind got the best of your hair right before a big meeting. Or maybe it's a cheap tourist sweatshirt purchased out of frigid desperation on a trip to the nation's capital. Whatever the circumstances, whatever the object, there's a time, and a power mindset, to help you let go. "I'll Get Something Better" is best applied to objects that you haven't used for at least 90 days.

You'll find yourself using this mindset as you dig deeper into closets and explore rooms you haven't entered in days. You find items that you cherished enough to store safely, along with, the same reasons to keep it again. With each item you find during your practice, assess the last time you used it and the potential for using it in the next 90 days. If you haven't used something for 90 days, its purpose to you has dissipated into clutter. Be thankful for what it has done for you and open your space by removing it from your home. If you do need it again in the future, you'll be able to replace it with something better than what you had.

Power Mindset 3 - "Clinging To An Item Lowers Its Value"

In college, I impulsively bought a dress from one of the big fast-fashion brands during a shopping trip with one of my best friends. The first time I wore it, I received a multitude of attention and compliments. I relished the confidence I felt, especially as an awkward college freshman trying to find my way. It's been years since college, and even more time has passed since the shopping trip that delivered such a dress. Yet, it remained in my closet. When integrating my possessions into my new home, I felt the weight of dragging the dress with me wherever I went. All of the warm fuzzy feelings I used to feel when holding the fabric in my hands were replaced by feelings of weariness. I was weary at having carried it with me for so long and weary from the crushing reality of the project I was taking on with my new home. The value this dress held for decades deflated faster than a bunch of balloons in a nail factory.

By clinging to this dress, I diminished its own value. The truth is, if you hold onto everything because it is special, then nothing is ever *uniquely* special.

Practicing this power mindset may seem daunting. There are countless birthday cards, letters, gifts, memorabilia, and more tugging at you. It's important to remember, however, why you began this journey. You might be looking for a new start. Or you felt that clutter was beginning to control your life. Whatever the reason for starting, we're all looking for the same effect: peace, clarity, and serenity. These are the direct results of practicing minimalism. Keep them in mind as you practice and pair it with each power mindset, to reach the goal you've set for yourself.

90/90 Rule

These power mindsets lay the foundation for your approach to clutter in your home. As you get into your practice, there's one more tool you should keep close: the 90/90 rule.

Joshua Fields Millburn and Ryan Nicodemus share this rule on their blog, The Minimalists, and iterations of it can be found elsewhere. When holding an item, ask yourself the last time you used it. If it has been more than 90 days and you don't see yourself using it in the next 90 days, then it goes. Letting it go means that the space it occupied is now clear and if you do find you need it in the future, you can get a better one.

This rule also acts as a thread of motivation throughout the practice of minimalism. Even if you are approaching your home in small increments, you are still prone to being overwhelmed. By having this rule at the ready, you can quickly decide if a random object is worth keeping or not. The prospect of getting a new one in the future, should you need it, also makes the rule easy to apply. So many consumer products and tools get better over time. Chances are you could find a higher quality replacement at a lower cost, should you ever need an item again.

Family Heirlooms

We've gone through the junk drawers, closets, under-bed storage, and can even see a clean garage on the horizon. But in all of those places, family heirlooms lurk demanding attention. These objects can be some of the most emotional to part with and let go. We often feel a sense of responsibility for these objects and that the burden is on us to preserve them for the next generation. To help you sort through family heirlooms, I've created several categories of items and how to approach organizing them or giving them away.

China, Flatware, and Other Dining Ware

If you are the recipient of a china set, flatware, or various kitchen utensils and tools, congratulations! These may be some of the more useful family heirlooms to receive. However, staring into the pattern of a dessert plate with the intentions of throwing more gatherings is not the same as regularly hosting more events. Sort through each piece and see how it might replace an item you currently own or how it would add to your routine. Consider also where it would live when not in use. Assuming you won't be using bone china with gilded edges as everyday plates, you want to store what you keep in an accessible location. You also want to make sure it doesn't crowd the items used on a daily basis.

Clothing, Jewelry and Accessories

Vintage clothing, jewelry, and accessories are constantly coming back into style. You may have several pieces, pillbox hats, 50's baubles, or a Pendleton suit that were once part of a family member's wardrobe. Clothing like this may especially be difficult to part with because you might have memories of the person wearing it and they're no longer here. Unless these items can fit into your current wardrobe and style, it doesn't make sense to store them indefinitely. There are many people who wear vintage clothes exclusively and would love the chance to own these items. Feel confident knowing those people will take pride in wearing the items and take care of them. Local vintage stores or even a consignment store can take these items for you and do the heavy lifting of finding their new owners. If your supply is dense and you have the time, you may also want to open an online store on an existing platform to list and sell the items. Donating to the costume shop of a local theatre or school's art program would also find new life for these items.

Furniture (Both Small and Large)

Furniture styles range so drastically just in the last 100 years. Mid-century modern was sold at the same time another furniture maker was reviving Queen Anne style dining chairs. If you receive furniture, large or small, carefully consider their purpose and how they might be of help to you in your organized home. A secretary desk may replace one you currently own and provide proper storage for everything in your home office. A tall buffet that used to hold China may serve you better as a bookcase in a reading nook you set up for yourself.

If there are pieces that don't match your decor or won't be able to serve a purpose in your organized home, it's okay to let it go. Depending on the style and condition, there may be specific collectors who would love to own the pieces. You can contact a local antique dealer for help finding a buyer or if you would like to make a philanthropic gesture, donate the furniture. Organizations that build homes for low-income families can sell the furniture to support their mission or place them into the homes themselves.

Home Decor

This category can be expansive. Vase collections. Plant stands. Paperweights galore. Since there are so many elements of home décor, deciding which ones to keep can be daunting. If you've inherited these items you've received little pieces of the home your relatives made for themselves. This in no way means you need to assume their aesthetic as a way of honoring them. Find what fits into your style and what you can realistically house. Then, let the rest go.

Chapter 2. Minimalist Shopping

How To Transform Your Spending Habits

As I talked about in the introduction, this book is about finding the balance between the objects you own and your intent. An essential part of maintaining that balance is to transform your spending habits.

As I began the process of decluttering my home, a heavy thought hit me: What's to stop the house from filling up again with *more* things? The halls of consumerism surround me everyday. The grocery store now sells seasonal home décor. A simple trip to a big box store to check off my list of needs turns into a mental war against bringing home every other thing I see. I needed to do more than I'd ever done to ensure my practice of minimalism in this new home was not in vain. In this chapter, I put together the best ideas to avoid the pitfalls of consumerism and ensure success in your own practice.

The average American household spends $18,000 each year on nonessentials. This includes everything from subscription boxes of beauty goods to expensive dinners. We buy new outfits for a special occasion despite already owning several that would suit. We let ourselves wander through the bargain area at the front of our favorite big box store only to walk away with handfuls of goods. We upgrade items in our homes not because the old version is broken, but because it is no longer the newest model.

Our collective habit of consumerism opens the flood gates to clutter in our homes. You may often find yourself receiving a new Amazon box before you've even had a chance to recycle the one you received just last week. You upgrade your blow dryer because you found a good deal and decide to hold onto your old one "just in case." Before you know it, your drawers and cabinets are full. Your mind begins to lose the peace and serenity of an organized home. You lose track of recent purchases amongst all the chaos of clutter.

It's not difficult to see the correlation between bringing things into your home and increasing the overall clutter. There is a financial side effect, however, that is both shocking and even a little upsetting: 60% of adults lack the savings to cover a $1,000 expense. This is a direct result of Americans' yearly spend on nonessentials. The most worrisome part of this statistic is that a $1000 expense is not wholly uncommon. A car repair or unexpected medical bill could easily hover around that mark. A much-needed home repair or appliance breakdown could also wipe out limited savings. I have dealt with my own fair share of new car brakes and lawnmower breakdowns. It was impossible to handle those unexpected expenses without my savings.

I don't bring all of this up to scare you or discourage you from your practice. On the contrary, these numbers should encourage you on your journey. I want them to motivate you to continue what you started and affirm your decision to take the momentous step of opening yourself to modern minimalism. Our modern consumer-based culture is at odds with minimalist living, it's an enemy of the practice. The financial consequences impact not only your wallet, but your peace of mind. The peace and serenity sought from practicing minimalism is crushed under the weight of the consumer mindset pressed upon us. Acknowledging that and carrying it with you through your practice protects you like a piece of armor.

Shop and Buy With Intention

One of the lasting childhood memories I have of my late mother is shopping. Sometimes it would just be a trip to the grocery store to pick up our staples for lunch and dinner throughout the week. Occasionally it would be a quick trip to the mall for new gym shorts. A particularly exciting shopping adventure happened every year, right at the end of summer. We'd pack up in the family van and drive to the local outlet mall to cover our back-to-school shopping. We had our list of stores we'd visit each year and depending on what we found each time, we'd cut a few from the list for that year. I looked forward to the fresh start of a new wardrobe each year and it was justifiable to meet the needs of my growing body. As I got older, I still loved the tradition of a yearly trip to the mall for several new items to add to my closet. I was even envious of a cousin who went to New York City each summer for new clothes.

Before I began my practice of minimalist living, I let the behaviors from childhood seep into my adult lifestyle. My voracious love for new clothes extended into all aspects of my adult life. New jobs meant new office supplies. A new year at college meant a new backpack and all new school supplies. But as an adult, the purchases didn't produce the same warm fuzzy feelings they did as a kid. Beyond the purchases necessary for living, everything else felt like a one-time high that quickly faded. It left behind way too many things and a closing in feeling that comes from having too much stuff around you.

The fact is we have to shop. We need to shop for food to eat, clothes to wear, and sometimes begrudgingly, a new car when ours gives out. But, that doesn't mean you need to give up practicing minimalism. I turned my own shopping habits around in my pursuit of a minimalist home and put together the 8 rules I live by to keep my home clutter-free.

Rule 1: Unsubscribe and Unfollow Retailers

It used to be easy to avoid the trumpet calls of our favorite stores. Those emails we received en masse from giving out our email at the register or online checkout could just be deleted. We could unsubscribe from the list and call it a day. Now, we need to do that and more. Every brand leverages the channels of social media to promote their products as well as that 4-letter angel's call: SALE. Instagram, Facebook, and even

Twitter are flooded with aesthetically captivating content from brands. They want you to reach into your wallet and immediately put in your credit card number for the latest fad or gadget.

The easiest way to remove the temptation is to unfollow brands and stores on all social media platforms. Yes, the sponsored ads they pay for will continue to pop up here and there. But, with constant updates on their feed, you're missing so much content that could tempt you into buying something you don't need.

Another option to take this rule a step further is train social media platforms on the ads you don't want to see. On Instagram, when you spot a Sponsored post, you can tap the three dots in the upper right corner of the post and select "Hide Ad." Instagram will provide you with a few feedback options and you can select "It's Not Relevant." This method will not get rid of every single Instagram ad, but it will help cut down on the brands that are your pressure points. The brands that you know grab you with their semi-annual sales or the ingenuity of their product line.

On Facebook, you can repeat this method in much the same way. Find a sponsored post, select the three dots in the upper righthand corner of the ad, and a drop down menu will appear. "Hide Ad" is the first selection and when you tap it, the ad will immediately disappear and Facebook records the request. A small pop-up will appear and you can select your reason for hiding the ad.

Rule 2: Stay Away From Cute Shopping Areas

They're an epidemic. Main Street Downtown in Anywhere, USA is full of endless enticing window displays. Handmade signs call out at you to "shop local!" and check out the newest wares. They almost beg you to let go of shopping guilt because everything is locally made, fairly traded, and did they mention organic? I live between two amazing downtown areas with everything I could ever want. But, I stay away on almost every occasion and have a strategy to minimize my time walking the historic brick sidewalks.

My strategy involves parking and utilizing it to keep me from spending extra time downtown. I often need to visit a government office or drop off library books, but there's no reason for me to spend additional time exploring the shops. I typically choose a parking spot (or pay for one!) that is the minimum time I need to complete my business downtown. Knowing there is a literal clock running, I complete my errands and return to my car. There's no time to see what's new at the kitchen store when I see parking enforcement making their usual rounds.

When I visit friends and family in larger cities, cars are a hassle. I like to take public transit to most every destination within a city. To help me avoid the same temptation in larger cities, I will keep an eye on the timetable for the bus or metro and try to complete any errands or necessary purchases in time to catch the next bus or train. I can adjust it based on my needs for each situation and it keeps me accountable.

Rule 3: Research What You Want to Buy

Part of buying with intention is knowing what you plan to purchase. It's imperative that in the buying process you learn as much as you can about the product you need to own. This will allow you to assess a potential purchase's added value to your home. Each item you bring into your home now should serve you well in its life.

Before I begin my online research or even asking friends who have purchased a similar item, I think about the pros and cons for purchasing it. I often find after completing this list I lack the real concrete use this item will fulfill. It's saved me from many purchases that would have served me poorly.

Internet marketing can sometimes add to the temptation of impulse buying. Advertisers on the web use cookies to track our movements. When we visit an Amazon page to look at reviews or go straight to the website of the brand of item we wish to purchase, they know. They use that knowledge to put banner ads on web pages we visit long after we've viewed their item. It's important to know this marketing tactic in order to stay accountable even when those pesky banner ads appear. Depending on your browser, you can even conduct your research using "incognito mode." This would allow you to search without the cookies being able to track your clicks when you return to the regular browser view.

Rule 4: Wait 48 Hours To Purchase

Good things come to those who wait. I'm a firm believer in this statement and find it best applies to minimalist shopping. I like to save the impulsive behavior for budgeting a vacation and choosing a destination at the last minute.

Waiting to make a purchase after you've decided on an item prevents you from regretting a purchase later. By not waiting and allowing the potential for regret, you may find yourself spending even more time by having to return it if it doesn't work out. Allowing yourself the space to think about your decision means you can weigh the purchase with a level head. It's easy to feel pressure to purchase something when a good deal comes up or when you find the perfect solution to an organizational problem in your home. Taking the time to let the decision rest will give you peace of mind and confidence when you do go to purchase the item.

Rule 5: Assess Your Buying Intentions

This rule takes the previous one a step further. Practicing modern minimalism requires a lot of intention. You're being intentional when it comes to what remains in your home and you should do the same with what enters. Whenever I want to purchase something new to bring into my home, I sit down and ask myself a few important questions.

Do I want this item because it will help me in my everyday life? How did I first decide I wanted this item? Did I hear an ad, see a sale, or hear about it from a friend? Do I own anything like it already that would serve the purpose I need?

The purpose of these questions isn't to interrogate yourself with every potential purchase. Instead, they're meant to get down to the core of your desire for the item. Practicing modern minimalism means we live with our best intentions, both for our home and for the items we bring into it. We all know the questions to ask ourselves to get to the root of why we desire what we do. Pulling those out while you're in the midst of shopping will ensure your potential purchase adds value to your life.

Rule 6: Make A List and Stick With It

I use this rule on a weekly basis. I make a list for my groceries and lists for trips to the bulk items store. The purpose of making a list is to help you stay accountable when you're standing in front of the attractive product displays or enticing checkout shelves.

My grocery list is ongoing, but when I plan a trip to the hardware store or a specialty store, it's usually for a specific project. I can often put together my rough list of items needed to complete a task thanks to research done beforehand. However, I prepare for any recommendations from store staff on items needed to do a job well.

After researching and taking time to think it over, don't let the lack of a hard list prevent you from walking past the impulse buys.

Rule 7: Use Cash or an Expense Tracking App

Cash is often touted as a way to keep better track of your spending and it can work well for many people. If you're like me, however, everything goes on plastic. I use my debit card almost exclusively to avoid ATM fees. Also, I don't spend as much as I would if I had cash burning a hole in my wallet.

For those who do use cash, it gives you an instant understanding of exactly how much you have and what you're spending. It can be more difficult to hand it over for something you picked up on a whim. Using cash also means change, which can be collected to fund a trip or an experience in your own backyard.

If you're interested in money tracking apps, there are a number out there and many of them free. Some banks even include the service as part of their online banking feature. Whichever app you choose, they all have their own features meant to keep you accountable. Pie charts, notifications, alerts, and plenty of design elements with bright colors keep your mind on your money and help you avoid impulse purchases.

Rule 8: One In One Out

I saved the best rule for last. This rule is key to helping you keep up your practice. It stands on its own as well as acts as a backup if you miss any of the previous rules. When you bring something home, find something else to take out of your home. This allows you to maintain the balance you've worked hard to find and keeps down the clutter.

It's not a crutch for bypassing the rules above. Simply cycling items in and out of your home to maintain a minimalist façade will be fruitless if your consumer habits remain unchanged. Do not fall into the trap of replacing your holiday decor each year because of a good deal or finding a new design more appealing.

The 8 rules above will help you in the shopping process. Whether its everyday shopping at the grocery store or a special trip to a furniture shop several hours away, keep these rules with you to support your practice of minimalism. When it comes to purchasing something new, I have another set of rules to help you.

Buying with Intention

This section is a set of questions to ask yourself about the item or items you'd like to purchase. We covered finding right intentions in the previous section, but these questions are here to help with the practical side of purchasing something new for your home.

Question 1: Is This Item a Need or a Want?

There are many items we see for purchase everyday. Our desires grab at different ones and it's important to distinguish if an item we want fulfills a need or a want. An item that fills a need will typically serve an active purpose. You most likely don't own it already or the item you had that served the purpose is broken. An organizing tray for your bathroom drawer will actively sort and separate bathroom items for ease of access. A new broom with dustpan will actively help keep your home clean. A new decorative plate or figurine collection might not actively serve a purpose and should be considered more carefully.
Or maybe altogether forgotten.

Question 2: Is This Item Something You Love?

An item you love will hold a higher place in your heart and home than one you just picked up for convenience. You may find need for a new broom and dustpan, but you may not love the one that happens to be in the cleaning aisle at the grocery store. Go back to the purchasing section, do your research, and find one you love with the features you need. Loving an item that you purchase will also serve you well as you care for it and put it to good use. A special occasion dress you adored and purchased to replace one that is worn out will benefit from the love you had for it in the dressing room. You'll keep up the proper dry cleaning schedule after wearing and store it lovingly.

Question 3: Where Will This Item Live?

This question should be easy to answer the farther along in your practice. Allowing space in your home for changing needs is a happy side effect of minimalism. Consider the space an item should live in. A new lamp for reading might be obvious, but where should you store sports gear that needs to be accessible throughout the year? Determining where a new item should live may even take some rearranging of your current organization. Take that into consideration and make those moves before you bring your new purchase home. If you live in a small space and need to purchase a larger item, consider alternatives to buying such as renting or using items available for use at a designated place in your neighborhood. On the other hand, you may have committed to a particular exercise routine and would like to bring the equipment into your home. In that case, weigh the positive impact on your health with the setup of your space and make the necessary adjustments.

Question 4: Will You Use It Often?

Continuing the example of new exercise equipment, it's important to honestly assess how much use you will gain from a new item purchased. Someone who is already committed to a cycling class 3 times a week will gain more from owning their own stationary bike than someone who tried a class once, but loved it. When gauging how much you might use something, I suggest trying before you buy. A new kitchen gadget sounds like a useful addition to your home, but could be just another item to store if you don't use it. See if a friend has the model you're looking to buy and try it out. Find your favorite exercises that keep you coming back before bringing home gym equipment.

Keep in mind, however, that whatever you bring home will require its own maintenance, cleaning and storage. That's additional time taken away from other parts of your life.

Question 5: Do You Own Anything With a Similar Purpose?

Oftentimes the needs we have that require a purchase can be met by something we already own. You may have an empty plastic bin that would be perfect for the sweaters you're trying to store. A rarely used lamp in one room can turn into an active source of light by moving it to another room. Carefully consider the items you already own to see if anything would provide a sensible solution to your need.

It goes without saying that you can consider the above for each household member, not just yourself. Oftentimes, when you progress from impulse buying for your own needs, your brain can switch to the needs of others. You see a pair of shoes you know your friend was looking for and they're her size! There's the exact phone case your partner wanted and it's on sale. Even if you're avoiding stores and unsubscribing from retailer emails, these items can find you and grab you.

One household member to keep in mind is the four-legged kind. Cats and dogs are common pets requiring their own set of items to stay healthy. Cats love to play out their hunting instinct with toys and need to keep their nails in check with good scratching surfaces. Dogs need leashes, toys, beds, and more to keep them satisfied. It's important to care for your pets and provide the items they need. Then, avoid unnecessary trips to pet stores. If at first you find it difficult to ignore the calling of the newest chew toy, find a new way to get pet necessities. Several pet and big box web retailers offer subscription services to deliver food, treats, and litter on a set schedule. The service helps you avoid adding extra items to your cart and frees up the time spent going to the pet store. There is more packaging and transportation involved when items are delivered to your house. Consider the needs of your family and if you can transition back at some point in your minimalist practice to pet store shopping.

The tips and rules in this chapter are not meant to restrict you or lessen your excitement about shopping. On the contrary, they're intended to inject more joy into bringing something new into your home. You should bring home items that you're proud of and will help you in your home. You put in time, as well as, effort to find these necessary items, so each one should receive the highest standard of care and shine wherever it lives. By adopting these principles when it comes to shopping and buying new items, you avoid the trap of creating more clutter.

Chapter 3. Living Room

Decluttering Strategies That Will Inspire You

The living room looks different in every home. In smaller homes, it occupies little space in order to share with other rooms and their adjoining functions. In larger homes, there may be formal and casual living rooms that stand on their own. In any scenario, a living room lives up to its name. It's meant to hold the life that goes on in the home. It's often the space where you spend most of your time, outside of the kitchen. It contains space for your family to gather together, including pets. Practicing modern minimalism in the living room can yield the greatest benefit because the open and stress-free space promotes harmony while minimizing conflict. With less physical clutter in the living room, mental space expands while energy increases.

Interior Designer Nate Berkus once exclaimed "In a minimal interior, what you don't do is as important as what you *do* do!" That is to say, those minimal interiors you peruse on Pinterest didn't happen by accident. They're the product of intention and effort. It takes more than white-washing walls and adding in sleek modern furniture. It's about making the physical space for your mental space. In the living room, that means finding the style you want to present yourself and your guests. I've put together practical tips for this chapter to help you remove the physical clutter and open up your space to achieve your minimalist goals.

The Living Room Game Plan: 12 Steps

Before getting started, make sure to remove extraneous objects from your living room. Some items may be better suited to other areas, but many things should be looked at and taken out of your living room completely.

1. Find a Wall Color That Brings Light

White walls reflect light the best and ignite an instant feeling of cleanliness and calm. White is an especially impactful color in the living room because of the many activities that take place there requiring light. It is perfect for reading, working on a puzzle or conversing with a gathering of friends. Having a wall color that reflects light back into the room helps your living room live up to its full potential.

White isn't the only option for your living room. Depending on your design, you can opt for a light color in purple, gray, or yellow hues. If you're going to go with a color other than white, keep that in mind as you put your room back together with furniture and decor. The point is to find what works for your style while still providing a calm background for the room.

2. Keep Decorations Simple

The decor in a living room shouldn't distract from the life that goes on within its walls. It can and should follow a theme that threads together throughout the room. Avoid mixing and clashing styles of items to keep the mental space open. If there's a bookcase, avoid stuffing every shelf full of books. Instead, choose select books that are often used or discussed and place them amongst the shelves. Leave space between clusters of books to break them up aesthetically and avoid overwhelming the shelf.

Other surfaces should remain mostly free to allow for temporary uses. A tray of appetizers or drinks during game night can easily find a place when you don't clutter surfaces with decor. Fireplace mantles or floating shelves are decor elements themselves and can provide additional space to draw attention to particular decor items. In addition to keeping the physical space clear for your mind, you'll find it easier to display holiday decorations.

Practical items like remote controls for TV's or monthly periodicals waiting to be read can find homes on a shelf of a side table, in a basket, or in a drawer in a piece of living room furniture. This keeps them within reach without being part of the decor.

Mixing design styles in the living room to put everything you hold dear on display will distract from those special pieces. By ordering your decor into one theme, you can easily draw attention to your style and the pieces that are important to you.

3. Add Texture

With smooth walls and clear surfaces as a base, you can introduce texture into the room in a variety of ways. Find pillow covers with larger than normal loops in the weave of the fabric. Opt for a velvet couch cover or one with a woven fabric. Find a rug that sits between low pile and shag that's easy to maintain but still offers texture.

You might even forego a color on one wall and pattern it with a removable wallpaper that has texture. In the absence of a textured wall, consider the artwork you'd like to hang and opt for something bold and structured. Texture is a special element to add to your living room exhibiting warmth. It can even enter the room through the light fixtures.

4. Make Special Furniture the Star of the Show

The living room is the place for your statement piece of furniture to shine. The chaise lounge you inherited from a family member. The one-of-kind coffee table made out of walnut with a live edge. The living room can be the launching pad for this prized furniture and stand out amongst the sleeker design elements.

A statement piece of furniture in the living room garners the attention it deserves from the frequent use of the room. Guests can appreciate it more often while you have the pleasure of using it in your everyday life. In order to keep the space open when displaying your piece, minimize decor elements around it. If it's a seat of some sort, keep pillows or blankets to a minimum and simple in design. If it's a coffee table, avoid cluttering it up with magazines or other items. The salvaged mantle with aged wood grain shines best without cluttering it to the point it looks like any other shelf you might have installed.

5. Share Your Style

The living room doesn't have to be devoid of your personal style. Choose an element that defines your personal style and integrate it into the room. If natural color wood is a design element you love and defines your style, add it to the room. Maybe your style is big and bold, like pops of bright color in the decor pieces.

Your living room is an extension of you and should be treated as such when organizing and decorating the space. Tying your personality into the details of the room is part of what makes it a calm and peaceful place. It's what will make friends and family say "Yes, that's you!" when they come to visit.

6. Use Greenery for Softness

Whether you stick with clean lines throughout the space or add in texture, there's always room for some softness, too. Plants are an excellent way to add greenery and a soft element to the room. You can even find plants that specialize in cleaning the air. If you're worried about keeping plants alive, especially while traveling, consider succulents that require less water but still offer the soft texture.

It's easy to add plants without taking up surface space, whether on furniture tops or the floor itself. Simple plant hangers make it easy to add plants without cluttering up the floor. They draw your eye up to see the expanse of the room and when hung at the right height, are easy to keep watered.

7. Make A Difference With Subtle Color

If bold colors are not part of your personal style, consider adding subtle color through items like books, a collectable vase, or even a blanket in the seating area. Staying in the same color family adds visual interest while displaying the items you want those visiting your living room to see.

You can also add color using the softer elements of your design. Curtains, pillows, and even upholstery can carry soft color throughout your room.

8. Embrace the Dramatic

The style and architecture of your home may lend itself to drama in the form of intricate baseboards, door frames and custom built-ins from another era. Whatever elements your home provides, you can play up the drama with items like dark toned curtains or a dramatic color for your couch. The point is, with all the work you've put into organizing and going minimal within the living room, you've now made space for drama.

9. Highlight Your Art

The living room is the perfect place to display your favorite art. Not only will it receive the appreciation of guests, but more admiration from yourself as you spend more time in the space. In a clean and minimal living room, your art can take center stage while other elements remain simple. It doesn't need to take up an entire wall either. If you have a piece or series of pieces that can be framed to match, a mantle or other shelf may be the perfect place to display it.

No matter the media, you can get creative in hanging and displaying. Hidden frame hangers that attach to the wall behind the art may be best for some pieces. For others, displaying elongated wires hanging on nails might fit the design of the room better. Even still, a simple picture shelf hung the length of a couch may be the right fit for the room.

10. Focus On Smaller Decor Elements

Chances are, you're not reading this book to complete a full overhaul of each room in a weekend. The focus is on reducing clutter and while that is achievable in every room, new furniture and decor in every room may not. Don't worry. Take the design elements that are the easiest to change out: paint, curtains, even a slipcover for the couch/chairs and turn them to neutral to contribute to the feel of minimalism in the room.

Your home may have older wood floors in patterns no longer offered or you're still holding onto a retro couch because it's in great condition. Whatever the case, you can find ways to modernize and quiet loud patterns. Find a simple monochromatic rug to cover part of the old floor.

Cover up the bright 90's floral pattern on your couch with a slipcover from the store or your linen closet for an instant calm.

11. Highlight Views or Patterns

If your living room happens to feature an amazing view, run with it. The mountains, trees, or even a city unfurling before you all capture attention and make a great focal point in the room. You can place furniture to take full advantage of the view while minimizing decor around the window or windows.

If you're in an apartment with windows facing other windows or don't like the view out of your living room, get creative. Use patterns in the wall decor to draw the eye to a view of your own creation. A set of black and white photos with matching frames would work perfectly. Or a triptych of a pattern spanning a large section of a wall will garner attention.

12. Bring In the Light!

The living room is used at all hours of the day. Take into consideration the additional light you'll need at night. Also consider the cloudy days and the times when the sun isn't bursting through the windows and doors. You may need a lamp for reading in your favorite chair or lounger. If you lack overhead lighting, consider adding fixtures to the walls in even numbers to add light and keep the design smooth. Wall light fixtures also save floor space keeping the open and calming feel you want for the space. You don't need an electrician, either. Many wall fixtures are wired. With a little paint and hardware, you can affix the wires to the wall and avoid the intrusion of a tangled wire mess.

There's a bonus step that will apply to most homes, but not all. This step calls for you to make space for pets. Cats and dogs require space and even furniture to keep them comfortable. Consider them when planning out the space and take advantage of new furniture designs with more than one purpose. If your living room is small and includes the entryway into your home, consider a bench that conceals a litter box underneath. If you have a strict "no dogs on the couch" policy, find a stylish pet bed in their size to work into the design and flow of the space.

If you have fish or other terrarium-dwelling pets, consider making their home the focal point of the room. Focus on their housing and design to draw attention not only to them, but their stylish habitat. A minimalist living room with pets will look different from a minimalist living room without pets. That's okay, though, because pets provide their own kind of mental benefit and inspire peacefulness with their unconditional love.

These 12 steps will apply differently to each person depending on personal style and taste. It's also important to consider the shape and size of your living room.

This book is for you to make your own and it's up to you to decide what elements work best in your space. These 12 steps are a guideline to help you as you continue to practice modern minimalism. They're a reward in themselves for the hard work you're putting in to make your space the calm and serene retreat you deserve.

Chapter 4. Bedrooms

The Best Kept Secrets to Serenity

The bedroom is a sacred place in the home. It's where you rest and recharge to recover from the outside world. It should be an open space that supports meditation and better sleep. Modern minimalism supports this goal by cutting down on the clutter and turning up the calm. If you start the process with the understanding that the bedroom is the one place in your home to recharge, the rest is easy. I've put together 10 tips to achieving the sanctuary to inspire and rejuvenate. Take note of what is achievable right now and what you can plan for in the coming weeks and months. The bedroom is worth pondering over and planning carefully.

Before we get started with the 10 tips, I wanted to advise on the bedroom-specific clutter often found. Televisions are ever more popular in bedrooms especially as their price goes down and the screen size goes up. They can be distracting in the space, however, and should be relegated to a different room or disposed of altogether. Our laundry often finds its way into all corners of the bedroom. Instead of keeping a laundry hamper or basket in the bedroom, make space for it in the bathroom or closet. These are spaces where you're more likely to get dressed and undressed, anyway. Books and magazines often stack up on bedside tables, even after they've been read. Reading is a soothing part of a bedtime routine and in order to support it and maintain calm, keep the materials to a minimum. Find storage out of sight, in a bedside table drawer or a basket on the shelf of the bedside table. You'll want to keep your reading materials close, but still save surface space from the clutter.

Cash may no longer be king in terms of what you carry in your wallet, but loose change seems to always find its way to the dresser top. Minimize this by designating a place for it out of sight and regularly deposit coins at your bank to keep it from piling up. Jewelry trays that often catch the loose change and jewelry pieces worn that day should be removed and if possible, stored with your clothes in your closet. Consider investing in a low profile alarm clock to use in place of your phone alarm to disconnect further from the outside world. If an old school alarm clock isn't your style, utilize the do not disturb settings on your phone to block all notifications during a set time each night. Landline phones, much like TV's, do a wonderful job of keeping us up. Take care to minimize them in your bedroom sanctuary.

If you have pets, chances are they prefer sleeping in your bedroom with you. Consider them in the design of the space to support their needs. If your dog sleeps in a crate, consider one that can double as a nightstand to save space and add style. Cats often sneak onto your bed but can also prefer a bed of their own. Assess your cat's preference and provide the sleeping setup they need. Make sure your cats have access to their litter box and water, if you close your door at night. Careful consideration of your pets and their needs during the process of decluttering your bedroom prevents imbalance of objects down the road. You don't want to find yourself in the final stages of designing the space only to realize there's a scratching post that now has to find a place to live in the bedroom.

Choose a Calming Color for the Wall

Just like in the living room, start with the basics in your bedroom: wall color. There's a lot of research on the psychology of color and how it affects our moods and psyches. Keep that in mind when choosing a color in your bedroom. A creamy warmer white is always in style and gives you a blank canvas feel. With no distraction of color, your mind can clear itself of thoughts and worries to promote restful sleep.

Blue is another color suited for the bedroom. A lighter shade can perfectly compliment neutral beiges and tans found in other parts of the room. Its effect on your mood is a calming one, but not draining. Seek a shade that doesn't overpower the room with boldness, but one that sits just in the background putting out a constant air of calm.

Pink is the tranquil partner of the color red. It can be suitable for a bedroom in lighter shades that don't overwhelm the design. Dusty pinks can provide the tranquility of the pink family without being overbearing. If you consider this color for your bedroom, make sure to take into account the other elements to prevent color clashing.

Pick Out a Minimal Bed Frame

In order to keep your bed suited to its purpose, which is sleep and sex, consider a minimal bedframe. Trends in furniture design are slowly turning away from the clunky and chunky furniture from even a few years ago. Many retailers from big box stores to established furniture makers offer a selection of minimal bed frames. These pieces feature clean lines and neutral colors so the focus in your bedroom is on you and your rest.

You may also choose to go without a bed frame and utilize a standard metal box spring frame to give you a little elevation off the ground. Without the added element of a bed frame, your bedroom opens up even more and detracts less from its purpose. It can be easier to keep your room clean without a bed frame with no need to dust and cleanliness being just a load of laundry away. Whatever style you choose, carefully consider the size of your room and your sleeping needs when choosing a bed. A king bed in a small room may not make sense unless you're able to balance its size with restricting other bedroom furniture. You might install floating side tables to balance the floor space taken up by a larger bed. You could rely on other furniture being off the ground either with legs or with installation on the wall.

Select Neutral Colored Bedding

Now that you've selected your bed, it's time for soothing bedding. Your bedding needs will depend on the seasons where you live. You may use a top sheet or opt for the European style of just a fitted sheet. Your local climate may require a heavy quilt and comforter for part of the year or a light blanket year-round. Whatever the case, use the opportunity to dress your bed as one to supplement the calm in the bedroom.

One way to do that is with a monochromatic bedding scheme. All white or all beige brings focus not on changing colors from pillowcase to fitted sheet, but to a blank canvas. A blank canvas where your thoughts and dreams are free to roam. Depending on your need to keep clothing and other decor in your bedroom, bedding is a simple way to minimize and open the space.

Thread Neutral Tones Throughout the Room

With neutral bedding in place, continue to thread those tones throughout the room. Rather than have a statement piece of furniture like in the living room, try to keep colors in the same family. This will prevent the room from being overwhelmed with too many focal points. By keeping neutral colors running throughout the room, you're creating an open space for you to recharge. Clutter can come in many forms and color is one of them. Just like you can have too many physical objects, you can have too much color that distracts from the space's true purpose.

This is especially important to keep in mind when organizing your bedroom. Find matching furniture pieces or stain ones to match. Consider the color on your wall before bringing in furniture pieces and keep decor in line with the color and tones you choose.

Find the Right Lighting

Lighting in the bedroom is a delicate art. At night, blackout curtains may be necessary to keep environmental light from waking you. During the day, you want as much natural light as possible to encourage you to use the space for meditation and reflection. Starting with the windows, find treatments that suit your needs while also maintaining the minimal aesthetic. This may look like a double-rod setup to hold a sheer curtain as well as blackout curtains in a neutral color. It could also mean shades or blinds meant to cover the entire window to block out light as needed. Whatever it looks like for you, make sure to keep in line with the other design and color selections you made for the room.

After natural light, the next best lighting in a bedroom is soft warm light emanating from carefully selected and placed light fixtures. LED light bulbs are pretty much ubiquitous nowadays. In the absence of the typical older style light bulbs, LED manufacturers have stepped up with more choices in light tones. It doesn't need to feel stark or sanitary in your room. Look for LED bulbs that say "soft light" or use marketing language like "relax." Better yet, visit a local hardware store to see bulbs on demo and find the one that works for you. There's a perfect hue that allows for relaxation, meditation and calm activities like reading.

Display Artwork

A bedroom is a sanctuary, hallowed in your home. This is a chance to display art that inspires calm and elicits positive feelings. To avoid cluttering the bedroom with art, choose one piece to display. You can always change it out with another piece should you feel the need. By having one piece of art on display, you're contributing to the feeling of open space.

Placement of the art will depend on its medium (sculpture or canvas painting) as well as the setup of the room. If you opted to go without a bed frame, a canvas above your bed that evokes feelings of calm is perfect. If you have a beloved sculpture, a separate pedestal or a space on a dresser free of clutter would give it the recognition it deserves.

Find One Place to Display Mementos

Our bedroom is where we are most vulnerable. When we sleep, we let go of our defenses in order to restore ourselves for the next day. It makes sense to keep the other parts of our vulnerable selves in our bedroom. Black and white photos of relatives, a specially gifted perfume, dried flowers from a special day all hold a sacred place in your heart. It's important to give these items space in your bedroom, without letting them devolve into additional clutter distracting the room from its purpose.

To prevent cluttering of mementos, find one space in your bedroom where you can thoughtfully arranged the pieces that mean the most to you. A low profile floating shelf or a small section of a dresser top could serve this purpose. Carefully select the pieces you want to display and store the rest. You may feel the need to change out what is on display. Keeping these items to a minimum means you can swap out as you see fit.

Add Greenery

Pops of green work well in every room, but live plants in bedrooms are especially beneficial. You're breathing the air in your bedroom all night and even with a clean filter in your central air conditioning system, there's still plenty to be filtered out. Plants provide the benefits of electric air purifiers without sacrificing style and design. Utilizing the natural light in your bedroom, find a place to set up a minimal plant stand or take advantage of hanging options to keep your floor space clear.

While all plants remove CO_2 from the air, there are some in particular that are adept at cleaning the air indoors. Consider a spider plant or a bamboo palm for pure green. Dragon Trees or Chinese Evergreens also keep your air fresh. Visit your local lawn and garden store for suggestions from the experts on your particular area. Even if you have access to plants that require a lot of sun, it may not be the best choice for your climate and even the direction your bedroom windows face.

Choose Your Clothing Storage Wisely

In the absence of a closet that can hold not only all your hanging clothes but the clothes that need to be folded, you will have some clothing storage in your bedroom. In your process of minimizing the amount of clothing you own, you should be able to get the items of clothing down to a manageable level. The next step with turning your bedroom into a sanctuary is choosing the right furniture to store your clothes.

Ideally, you should be able to fit all your clothing into one piece of furniture. A taller chest of drawers takes up less vertical space and can draw the eye up. A shorter chest of drawers with a greater width can offer surface area for the proper lighting and minimalist storage of jewelry. You may need something completely different because of closet space or even the makeup of your wardrobe. You may need an actual wardrobe that has hanging space accompanied by a few drawers for the clothing items that absolutely need to be folded and stored. When you find what works for your needs, think about where it should go in the space to maximize its functionality. Stick with it. Place near a window for maximum light or next to the bathroom door to make dressing easier.

Minimalism Does Not Equal Cold

All of the tips and suggestions in this chapter will make a world of difference in your bedroom. They're exactly what you need to make your bedroom the calm and restful place you deserve. They help you pare down the excess to make room for the possibilities. That is what modern minimalism is about. It's not here to turn your home into a cold prison-like shelter devoid of warmth. It's here to open up your space which allows you to open your mind. You should have warmth in your bedroom and following the tips in this book will get you there.

Putting together your perfect minimalist bedroom is a reward that renews itself with each period of sleep. Your bedroom is an escape from responsibilities and everyday struggles. Your efforts to make the space reach these goals will be felt daily. Take it one step at a time and remember your goals for practicing minimalism. You're on your way to a bedroom and a home of your dreams.

Chapter 5. Laundry Room

The Game Changing Routine You Need

With how often you use the laundry room, it may seem daunting to apply minimalist principles to its organization and function. I argue that because of the high volume of use, it's the easiest room to implement a solid strategy for organization and functionality. The first step is to assess the space. Laundry rooms vary in size and can hold more than one function, such as a back entry to your home with a mudroom. If you're in a smaller space or live in a home designed to maximize square footage to other purposes, you may have little more than a closet. The closet may not even have storage and be completely taken up by machines. Whatever the setup, take a minute to analyze what you're using the room for currently.

Once you have an idea of how you're currently using the space, it's time to learn a new routine. These new habits make the most of the space and allow for you to keep the minimalist mindset you're practicing in the rest of your home. After reading and adopting the following routine, I'll lead you through the reorganization of the space to best suit your needs. Say goodbye to random piles of laundry and spilled laundry detergent. Say hello to clean lines and open space.

Habit 1 - Wash A Load Every Day

One of the biggest factors contributing to messy laundry rooms is a pile of dirty clothes ready to be washed. Allowing clothes to pile up and waiting for a specific day of the week to clean means that laundry day is the only day the room is truly clean. In order to maximize your efforts to create a modern minimalist home, adopt the habit of washing a load of laundry every day. Between sweaty gym clothes, sheets, blankets, and towels, there's plenty to wash on a daily basis. You don't have to be excessive in what you wash; jeans and dry-clean-only clothes typically don't need a wash after one wear.

If you do find yourself with too little to wash each day, consider washing every other day to keep the clutter to a minimum. If you find that many items are too delicate for the dryer, find a permanent setup for drying. Depending on your space, you could install a minimalist rack matching the color of the door to blend in and always be at the ready to dry clothes. You could also use any wall space in your laundry room to affix a simple rack in a neutral color, like natural wood. If wall or door space is not an option, find a smaller than standard folding drying rack that can be set up for the days you have delicates to dry. A smaller sized rack can easily hide between one of the machines or tucked behind a door.

Habit 2 - Don't Overfill with Detergent

If you're using liquid detergent, chances are you're using too much. Detergent formulas are heavily concentrated and using less than what the bottle says will still produce clean clothes. Overusing detergent also runs the risk of leaving residue on your clothes and irritating sensitive skin. Stick to just below the recommended line on the dispense cup and save money and plastic by not going through as many detergent bottles.

While liquid has long overtaken the market, powder is beginning to make a comeback. One of the benefits is its lighter weight and less packaging as compared to standard liquid detergent. Both of these features save on fuel for transport and thus can result in a lower price compared to liquid. In addition to being a bit more friendly to the environment, powdered detergent is much easier to store and keeps with the minimalist aesthetic. You can find a container that fits in with the design of your laundry room and avoid having the bright marketing colors of liquid detergent bottles distracting from a clean space. As a bonus, many manufacturers of powder laundry detergent set out to make formulas with less chemicals. This is a boon to those with sensitive skin and people looking for more natural alternatives to modern detergent ingredients.

Habit 3 - Cold Water is Key

Using cold water in all your wash cycles simplifies your work leaving space for your mind to focus on other things. Cold water not only works for delicates or heavy-duty textiles like towels, it also saves money. By foregoing the hot water, you're using less energy and reaping the benefits on your energy bill each month. Cold water is also excellent for a wide range of stains, including blood, whereas hot water can set those protein-based stains.

If you have greasy or grimy rags from cleaning, simply give them a hot rinse in your sink before throwing them in to wash. Cold water will help all your fabrics last longer and is especially useful for clothes, towels, and bedding. This simple habit dramatically impacts how you do laundry and reduces the costs associated with it.

Habit 4 - Sort By Color No More

Fabric dyes used in modern clothes are more likely to be steadfast and less likely to bleed onto other fabrics in the wash. Take advantage of this aspect of modernity and start sorting your clothes by the type of fabric rather than the color. By dividing clothing and linens by fabric, you streamline the number of loads and the cycle types needed. Most homes will use two cycles: delicates and regular. The difference is in the spin speed and is meant to support the longevity of more delicate pieces.

When you bring new pieces of clothing or other linens into your home, wash them once to test their steadfastness, especially if they're darker colors. A wash will also clean off dangerous manufacturing dust and leftover chemicals.

Habit 5 - No Need for Dryer Sheets

The last habit to adopt is getting rid of dryer sheets. Their benefit as a static remover is overshadowed by the chemicals present in them. Not to mention, the need to replenish stock on a regular basis eats into your wallet. Cut one more thing off your shopping list by getting rid of dryer sheets. If you're looking for an alternative to help with static and fluff up linens like towels, consider wool dryer balls. You can find them at big box stores and natural food stores. Toss a few in the dryer for each cycle and store them in a container that matches your laundry room aesthetic. Wool dryer balls last a long time and you won't have to worry about replacing them as frequently as dryer sheets.

By now, you can see how these habits build on each other. They each have a purpose on their own. Taken together, they're a new routine to streamline the work of your laundry room. By adopting this routine, you will cut down on the mental space devoted to a necessary household chore. This is especially beneficial as laundry is ongoing. The savings in your time, money, and energy stacks up quickly with these new habits.

Now that you've adopted helpful habits in the laundry room, it's time to set up the space to keep you successful in your new routine. I touched on helpful tools and storage ideas in the previous section, but in this one, I want to walk you through every aspect of a laundry room. By thoroughly assessing your needs, you can set up a space that is functional and easy to keep clean.

Step 1: Group Your Clothes

We only have as much laundry as we do clothes. It seems an obvious truth, but it doesn't really set in until you go from owning mounds of clothes to a few capsules of a wardrobe. With less clothing, you wear more and wash less. Rather than piling up a week's worth of clothing from wearing new pieces each day, you're wearing and washing the same items. This means there's no time for them to pile up on the floor or the laundry basket. If you're following the habit of doing a load each day, then you're able to keep the clothing clutter in your laundry room to a minimum.

Depending on where you live, you may have a wardrobe for each season. Grouping these items together either in your drawers, hanging in your closet, or stored in bins will simplify your routine. It will make getting dressed easier as well as helping you keep track of favorite items that are worn often, and thus, washed often.

Step 2: Carve Out Laundry Spots

So far, I've laid out the best habits for washing and drying laundry. But what about the steps that come before and after the wash? They're just as important and require strategic thinking to streamline the operation. It's time to consider the whole routine of laundry, starting with where you keep dirty clothes. Depending on the layout of your house, you might be able to take the dirty laundry you've just worn and deposit it into the laundry room. This is possible due to the rise in popularity of main floor laundry rooms that take advantage of a convenient water source (bathrooms!).

In the absence of laundry located conveniently next to the room where you undress, you'll more than likely have a hamper. If possible, you should try to find either a low profile hamper or make space in a bathroom cabinet for a basket to catch laundry. In either case, make sure it is easy to carry to and from the laundry room. Invest in two baskets or hampers of the same kind. Keep one in the laundry room, making it easy to transport clean clothes back to their home. Use the second basket in your bathroom to place dirty clothes.

After figuring out a way to store and transport dirty laundry efficiently, tackle the post-wash need for folding space. Reserve the counter space in your laundry room for this purpose. This way you can transport not only clean laundry to a dresser or closet, but folded laundry that's ready to be put away. If your laundry room lacks counter space, consider a folding table that's easy to set up. Some ironing board designs maximize surface space and could function as a folding table in addition to an ironing space.

If space is lacking for folding and ironing in your laundry room, consider moving the job to your closet or right in front of your closet. This will allow you to take clothes straight from the laundry room to a designated space where you can fold, iron, and put away. I mentioned a drying rack in the previous part of this chapter and want to bring it up again. If you're short on space, the back of a door or empty wall space would hold a rack perfectly. If that doesn't work in your space, consider a smaller drying rack that's easy to both fold and unfold. The advantage of a smaller rack is that if you do need to use it on a daily basis, it won't take up as much room and leaves more space wherever you set it up.

Step 3: Make the Most of the Space

Part of assessing your laundry room is discovering every area that may contribute to storage and organization. I've already mentioned the back of the door as an option, as well as the wall. With the right bins and containers, you can have everything you need to wash your clothes at the ready. If the door to your washer opens to the left, make sure the detergent is within reach on your right. If your appliances are stacked, take advantage of the additional accessible wall space and floor space to hang cascading baskets. You can keep wool dryer balls at the dryer level and detergent at the washer level. If you have space for closed storage, you can create clean lines and open space with ease.

If your laundry room is really just two appliances stacked to take up every inch of a closet with folding doors, don't worry. Invest in a mini rolling cart with a neutral color that can be organized to hold all your laundry supplies. You can even hook a mini drying rack on one end. With the supplies visible, consider containers to hold supplies that stay true to the theme of minimalism in your home. Containers lined with removable canvas or other fabric are great for accidental spills while opaque jars in varying sizes can hold everything from powder detergent, stain remover and a set of wool dryer balls.

Step 4: Upgrade Your Appliances

Speaking of appliances, consider upgrading the ones you currently have to ones that will better suit your space. If your space allows it, consider a stacking washer and dryer combo that saves on floor space and opens up wall space for built-in storage at your fingertips. Opting for a smaller capacity washer and dryer set helps support your new habit of washing a load each day. Newer washers sense how much water to use, but overall energy use decreases when you downsize your washer and dryer. You don't have to sacrifice the ability to wash bulky things with a smaller capacity set. You can simply separate bulky items like comforters or blankets to wash individually.

Smaller capacity sets tend to come with pedestal drawers. This additional storage space can make even the smallest laundry room more functional by keeping laundry necessities right where you need them. Newer machines will also be the most energy-efficient as standards are exceeded each year by manufacturers. Revel in the ability to lower your energy bills while still keeping your clothing, bedding, and other linens clean.

Step 5: Use Decor to Freshen Your Space

Decor in a room that's usually seen as strictly utilitarian may seem odd, but adding design elements can have a profound impact on the space. I want you to view laundry as not just a necessary evil, but a rewarding chore that can be bolstered along the way. Find a space in your laundry room, a doorway or even a section of the space, that can be divided by curtains. Adding a soft element can balance the hard lines of washers and dryers while serving a purpose as a room divider.

A new coat of paint can also freshen up the area, even if there is not a lot of open wall space. By removing everything from the room and painting a crisp white or even a calming lavender, you're elevating the space. Color can peek out where it can, while offering itself as a positive visual in the space.

Find a new area rug or runner to fit in your space. This will help pick up on loose lint before your next vacuuming, especially if you have hard surface floors in the space. In addition to a rug, add greenery for additional warmth. If your laundry room lacks natural light for plants, consider having two of the same kind to swap out. You can also invest in a high-quality silk plant if you don't want to fuss with switching plants from partial sun to no sun (and back again).

The laundry room is one of the rooms in the home that has a specific job to be performed. Rather than it being a place to live or sleep like the rooms I've already covered, its purpose is to keep the operation of living running smoothly. Efficiency, however, doesn't need to equal utilitarianism. A laundry room can be warm and inviting. It should support you in your chore of keeping the linens in your home clean.

With the proper habits established and the space outfitted to suit your needs, success is right at your fingertips. Enjoy the fruits of your labor with a clean laundry room and an empty hamper each night.

Chapter 6. Kitchen and Dining

Transformative Secrets

The kitchen, much like the laundry room, experiences a near constant flurry of activity. It's used daily and has a lot of accessories and appliances packed into what can sometimes be a very small space. No matter the size, a minimalist kitchen is meant to provide a clean slate every time you step in to prepare a meal or fix a drink. In this chapter, you'll discover ways to store, organize, and declutter your kitchen. With each step you follow, the possibilities of the space unfold before you. Imagine your reorganized kitchen as a space where the flow of activity is natural, items are exactly where they should be, and your mind is cleared of stress.

My kitchen allows me to sink into the therapeutic activity of cooking my favorite recipes and baking my favorite treats. A properly established minimalist kitchen will provide these same therapeutic effects to you. In the first section, I'll take you through the many categories of clutter we all have in our kitchens. In the last section, you'll find practical storage solutions for these categories. Taken together, these sections are transformative.

Step 1 - Declutter Small Appliances

It feels like every year there's a new must-have appliance for your kitchen. Air fryers, pressure cookers, rice cookers, slow cookers and more have found their way onto counters and never left. I am a true believer that no one person or family can make the best use of all the small kitchen appliances cluttering up counter space.

Before tackling the hoard of small appliances cluttering your kitchen, assess their use. Be honest with yourself about how often you use each appliance and how they truly benefit your lifestyle. If you're committed to early morning gym sessions and rely on your blender to give you the nutrients you need, keep it. If the rice cooker you bought after a trip to Hawaii inspired you to make rice at home, but now sits neglected, get rid of it.

The latest small appliances promise all sorts of new features to save you time and cook (mostly) healthy meals. Before considering a purchase, plan out how you would integrate an appliance into your kitchen routine. You can also apply this mindset to appliances you already have, but don't use. If there's one that tugs at you and seems like it would help you, try it out. Fit it into your kitchen routine for a week and see how it goes. If you don't use it at least half the time you prepare food in your kitchen, it's time to let it go.

Microwaves and toaster ovens are some of the most common small appliances. There are benefits to both, but I have found the benefits of a toaster oven outweighing those of a microwave. Microwaves distribute heat in a way that can leave your food flat or curdled (like eggs!). Toaster ovens take the power of a full-size oven and distill it into a smaller area. It can warm up food quickly, without dissolving its texture. Save on the electric bill by using a toaster oven and ditch the microwave.

Step 2 - Stick to One Set of Dishes

I see it on wedding registries of friends all the time. They pick out a 5-piece place setting for an everyday set of dishware and then want 12 or 16 sets! Inevitably, they never have a dinner party that big. If they do, it's way more than 12 people and requires paper or plastic ware to serve everyone. Keeping one set of dishes helps you avoid having the weight of unused items on your mind. Hold onto enough plates, bowls, silverware, and glasses for each member of the household, plus a few extra for guests. The extras are helpful, too, in case you break any in you original set.

By allowing only what you need to serve your household, you're helping boost the habit of washing dishes as you use them. This keeps your sink clean and keeps your dishwasher always ready for its next load.

I wanted to mention all of the miscellaneous dishware that can pile up when you're not looking. Travel coffee mugs, reusable water bottles, lids, straws, and more can end up cluttering your cabinets and not serving their best purpose. Assess your lifestyle and decide if you really need all of these accessory items around. A reusable water bottle is a must-have for me and I recommend keeping one on hand to use daily. Having it closeby helps you stay hydrated and healthy. If you lose it or leave it behind somewhere, you can always purchase a new one if you need to. Travel coffee mugs seem to be in every kitchen. However, if you're not on a long commute in the morning that where it is a necessity, you probably don't need them.

Knives are crucial to eating as well as cooking, but they should be selected for your kitchen with care. A good cook can get away with a lot using just a good quality chef knife. A paring knife is helpful for smaller foods like fruits. If you're feeding a larger family and have bigger cuts of meat in your recipes, a good quality carving knife is also important. If you tend to eat steak often, then a few steak knives would be appropriate. With having less knives, you can invest in better quality versions that will last and make food prep easier. As with each section of items in your kitchen, be honest with yourself about your lifestyle and the needs that go with it.

Step 3 - Keep Only Pans You Use

Retailers make it easy to come home with too many pans by packing up an array of various-sized cookware into one box for one low price. Chances are you won't be cooking meals that require that many different pans and in those quantities. A good retailer has high-quality cookware available for sale individually. Approach what you have currently with an individual mindset to pare down to exactly what you need.

To cook pretty much anything, build a small collection. This includes one omelette pan (between 10 and 12 inches), two saucepans (one large and one small), a stockpot, a strainer and a few lids. Any additional cookware should be kept or purchased only if it fits with your lifestyle. If the only way you eat vegetables is if they're steamed, only purchase the insert for one of your saucepans. If you use a cast iron skillet for sauteing food, simmering soup, or cooking steaks, use that in place of the traditional omelette pan. Some cooks swear by their dutch oven. If that's you, don't worry about the traditional stockpot. The point is to have just what you need and nothing you don't.

Step 4 - Limit Kitchen Tools and Gadgets

Kitchen utensils like spatulas and serving spoons are some of the most common counter clutter. When stored in drawers, they often shift around due to their unique shapes. when packed too tightly, they get stuck in the drawer. I advocate for as few utensils as possible to make your kitchen functional. This means a spatula, one slotted spoon, one soup spoon, one baking spatula, and a whisk. These utensils cover everything from cooking dinner to baking a cake.

Other tools like electric meat carvers or basting brushes are niche products that will only fit in if your lifestyle includes those methods of cooking. If you've been through a phase of making pastry and haven't touched the basting brush since, get rid of it. Make space for only what you do now in the kitchen.

Step 5 - Don't Overstock Food

Between membership warehouse stores to deep discounts on staples at the grocery store, it can be tempting to fill up the fridge or pantry with the deals we find. It's too easy to overstock when shopping for food because it's a necessity. It's easy to tell yourself you should stock up on soup because it's 10 for $10 because you feel you're going to eat it all eventually. But applying that logic to everything in the grocery store, leads to an overload of food. Before you know it, those snacks and boxed dinners are expiring because you never got around to eating them.

Use a membership warehouse to mainly purchase cleaning supplies, paper goods and plastic goods (like garbage bags). Try to only purchase food that you will eat within the week. This often means prepared meals, which saves time and is cost effective. At the regular grocery store, take advantage of the deals on food you consume regularly, but only buy what you need. I have found that the items I love buying go on sale on a regular basis. It doesn't make sense to stock up when another sale is just around the corner. By doing so, you're much more likely to be out or almost out of the food by the time the sale begins again. Compare this to just continually adding to the stockpile every time your favorite foods drop in price.

A good rule of thumb is to stock up on dry goods and shelf food, enough for a month, and then buy fresh ingredients weekly. Even better, purchase fresh ingredients every few days for your recipes. This ensures produce never goes bad and that you have enough of ingredients with a shorter life span (like dairy products). Grocery shopping every few days is not always feasible if the store is out of the way or your schedule makes it difficult to go on a 20 minute stop. However, for the support of minimalism, it is still a good goal to keep in mind

Step 6 - Clear Your Counters

Clean sightlines in a kitchen are instantly relaxing. Without the break in your line of sight caused by an appliance or dish rack, your mind stays focused on the tasks and day ahead of you. Rather than making the kitchen feel cold and unused, clearing as much as possible from the counters gives you a blank canvas. Whatever you decided to cook or bake is not limited by your prep space anymore. It's also easier to keep your counters clean if there are little to no obstacles to move when wiping them down. A clean kitchen starts with counters and when those are clear, you feel motivated to use the space. You immediately feel excited to transform a few ingredients into something spectacular.

I'll go over storage solutions in the next section, but start imagining the shift in your kitchen from moving things off the counter to a better space.

Step 7 - Make Visual Space

There are places in your kitchen where you may not be able to achieve a clear sightline. You need a helpful principle to apply throughout the cabinets and countertops. In this regard, it is best to leave open space between things not only for the modernist look, but for the modernist feeling. Being able to clearly see between items stacked in your cabinet or displayed on your counter makes the space feel bigger. That feeling is also absorbed in your mind. If your mind is seeing less clutter, then it *feels* less cluttered.

Step 8 - Find the Flow of Your Kitchen

If you're lucky, you have the perfect triangle. A perfect triangle is one that is drawn between the placements of the fridge, stove, sink. When those three stations are set up in such a way, you flow between them easily as you prepare, cook, and clean up. Most kitchens possess a triangle. This is the basis of your kitchen flow.

After that, the patterns in the kitchen often rely on the personality and habits of the household members. Find how you flow in your kitchen throughout the day. Start with making your first cup of coffee or tea in the morning and track your movements throughout the day. Over the course of a few days, you'll discover the pinch points in your kitchen. The places where things just don't work as well and should be changed. The coffee supplies are above the coffee maker, but that cabinet is right next to the stove which is really where you need the spices.

Consider the layout of the permanent fixtures of the space, like the triangle, and build stations around that. A prep station could have knives, cutting boards, mixing bowls all within reach while standing in one spot. A breakfast station could be right next to the fridge to make it easy to access juices and dairy (or non-dairy) products while assembling your non-refrigerated breakfast items.

Before we get into the second part of this chapter on the dining room, I want to share some practical storage solutions for the kitchen. These will help you clear your counters and simplify your cabinet storage.

Dry Goods and Other Shelf Food

If you're practicing dividing your kitchen into stations, think about grouping food or other shelf items together with their stations. Bread can be close to the toaster. Coffee and tea can be close to the french press or tea kettle. For all other foods, choose a cabinet or utilize the pantry to organize foods by group. Beans, rice, and pasta should go together. Jars and cans used for making pasta sauce should also be grouped in their own area. By grouping similar items, you're able to clearly see the stock you have and choose what you want based on the variety at hand.

Following the step laid out in the previous section, leave space between groups so you're not overwhelmed when you open the cabinet doors.

Knives

High-quality knives should not be in crowded drawers or in knife blocks. The best storage to maximize their longevity is a drawer with a non-slip pad for each knife to rest on separated from each other. Another alternative is installing a magnet bar on the inside of a cabinet door close to your prep area. This keeps knives safe and in reach when you need them.

Other Cutlery

Find a drawer close to the dishwasher or dish rack and use a divided organizer with non-slip silicone on the bottom, as well as inside the sections. This will keep the set of silverware from moving within the drawer. It will also keep the individual pieces stacked together with space between your forks, spoons, and knives.

Dishes and Glasses

When selecting the cabinet for dishes and glasses, you should consider where clean dishes are distributed from. Separate glasses from dishes to allow easy access to clean plates. If you have a variation in size of glasses, separate those again, but in the same cabinet. By grouping the sizes of glasses together you're making space between them and making it easy to identify what you need when opening the cabinet door.

Coffee and Tea Supplies

Group coffee, tea, mugs, and any accessories together for ease of use. If you keep favorite types of tea or coffee on hand, consider airtight containers to store them in. Immediately get rid of the original packaging. This helps make it easy to access your favorites and continue the minimalist theme in your storage solution. A cabinet would work well for these items. You can adjust shelves to different heights to be able to accommodate everything behind closed cabinet doors. This excludes a large coffee maker, which is best to remain stationed on the counter if used daily.

Kitchen Tools and Gadgets

Avoid keeping tools and gadgets stored on the counter. In addition to creating clutter, you're also exposing the clean tools to the dust in the air. Find a drawer where you can lay out a non-skid pad and set each tool in its own spot with space between. This way everything will stay in place each time you open the drawer and you can easily access the utensils.

Spices and Oils

Store these items close to the stove or prep area where they're often used. If you're using a cabinet to store them, consider step shelves to store spice jars on separate tiers. This makes it easy to spot what you need to use and keeps each jar in its place. Depending on your style of cooking, you most likely just need to have olive oil on hand. It does well in high heat, can add flavor to your food, and is often recommended for health benefits. Keep it close to the stove where you can easily access it when you're cooking.

Pots and Pans

Utilize the width and depth of under the counter cabinets to store your pans using their interior cabinet drawers. One drawer can hold pans while another can store lids. With only the pans you use on a regular basis, it's easy to fit them all into a single cabinet. This is more efficient than the two or more cabinets needed for larger collections.

Dining Room

A dining room is meant for gathering people and food. This space is meant to engage in shared experiences, as well, as creating new memories. A modern minimalist dining room supports that function through clean lines and open space. This allows the conversation and the company to fill the room, unobstructed by clutter. Below are 6 ways to usher your dining room into its next era.

Make Use of Large Open Space

Having a sizable open space for your dining room makes it easier to create the minimalist feel. It allows you to add necessary elements to the room without overwhelming the space. Emphasize the light flowing in from the windows and how it illuminates the space. Align the head of the table with the window. Draw the eye up to the high ceilings. All of these elements bring the peace and calm of modern minimalist design and organization.

In the absence of a large dining room, focus on elements that you can change to make it feel bigger. Adjust the height of the lighting if it hangs low so it's not in your immediate sightline. Consider purchasing a smaller table that can expand if you're a frequent host. Forego other dining room furniture like buffet tables or sideboards to keep the flow of the space clear and open. If you need these items, consider smaller versions that take up less space.

Neutral Colors

With wood being an oft-used material for dining room tables and chairs, you already have a great base for a neutral color palette in the space. Use browns, white, gray, and black to create an enlightening space instead of a distracting one. Decide if you want to thread the same color through all the major elements of the room or mix them.

If you decide to use a few colors, consider the combinations that work best together. An all white room is the epitome of clean and open. You may prefer to balance that, however, with infusions of black. This creates contrast and may make you feel less like you've created a void in your dining room.

Brown and white also balances well. If you have a dark brown wooden table and chairs, consider white seat pads, white walls, and a white sideboard to make the table the star. Lighter color wood, or furniture collections left in their natural state, also pairs well with white. Consider the trim on chairs or adding artwork to bring in this natural color to a white room.

Gray, especially lighter shades, can balance a white dining room or be the base as the color on the wall. You can even make it the focal point with a statement table made with a concrete top. Also consider gray accessories or art to balance with white. Blue can also work in your dining room either as a wall color or in the accessories and decor. Find the color that works best for your room and fits in the rest of your house. There are many options to suit your space.

The Right Lighting

Dining room lighting falls somewhere between bedroom lighting and kitchen lighting. You want to be able to see what you're eating and who you're with, but don't want to set a stark mood with too much light. An overhead fixture should provide ample soft light to create a special feeling while also allowing you to see what's on your plate. Accessory lighting could be wall mounted to emphasize a piece of art or simply highlight the height of the room.

For an overhead fixture centered over the table, consider hanging a little more above the sightline from a seated position. It would be higher than what you normally see in dining rooms, but would allow you to have a clear sightline from a standing and seated position as well as one from a seated position. If you're balancing the amount of light coming from this fixture, the added height should not interfere with the fixture's ability to illuminate properly

Functional Furniture

I mentioned tables with removable leaves in another section and want to highlight here as a perfect example of functional furniture. The ability to accommodate more than just the members of the household is important. You may be hosting a large family dinner or simply adding one more for a casual Saturday afternoon meal. Furniture design has offered this functionality for quite some time, but now there are more options in this realm. Dining tables now come with the ability to expand without having to detach a section of the table and find somewhere to store it. This supports your practice of modern minimalism by removing one more thing from the storage space in your home.

For the purpose of continuity, make sure to have additional matching chairs for your dining table. Attractive folding chairs now come in all styles. If you're storing them for most of the time to keep the minimal feel in the dining space, consider folding chairs instead of standard ones. Sideboards and buffet tables should provide storage to keep linens and candle accessories out of sight when not in use. Designs featuring clean lines and even hidden cabinet pulls will help maintain the minimal feel of the space.

Accent Walls

If you're keeping the contrast between colors to a minimum and have simply-designed furniture, consider an accent wall to spark your dining room. Taking a color from the neutral palette and making one wall stand in contrast to the others provides a backdrop to the furniture.

Use Patterns and Textures

Patterns and textures inject the room with warmth. Play with it by covering seat cushions in a pattern fabric or hanging a tapestry art piece on the wall. Find the places where you can add texture without overwhelming the space. A heavy velvet curtain could adorn either side of the windows. The food you're eating has texture, your dining room should, too.

There's a lot of information in this chapter and you'll see it is one of the longer ones in the book. Its length matches the importance of these two rooms. The place where we cook and the place where we eat are both worthy of great detail. Taking steps to declutter your kitchen will allow you to flourish within it.

By attaining a minimalist look in your dining room, you're opening the space to memories made while sharing meals with friends and loved ones. These rooms require careful thought and planning for all that they contain. The payoff, however, is felt everyday as you utilize both spaces.

Chapter 7. Minimalist Home Office

Essential Hacks

According to the Bureau of Labor and Statistics, the U.S. averaged 8.5 hours of work during the week. The 40-hour workweek is almost a dream at this point. With constant connection through smart phones and home offices, our work is integrated into our lives in new ways. How to make the most of that time can be difficult to determine. In this chapter, I'll walk you through the ways in which a modern minimalist home office supports productivity and help you organize the space to maximize focus.

The most productive minimalist home office has 3 things in common. There is less choice, less tools, and less friction. I'll share more detail below, but first I want you to imagine the more abstract concept of each quality. They all contribute to a more peaceful mind and they're qualities you wouldn't necessarily expect in an office. You may wonder what "less choice" has to do with productivity and how you're supposed to do your job with less tools. Step back and imagine working within a space that combines all 3. Imagine yourself less frustrated by choice, less encumbered by miscellaneous clutter, and how that supports ease of movement both physically and mentally.

Less Choice

The concept of having fewer choices in an office may not be the first thing you associate with a minimalist lifestyle. It's easy to build up an office as a space of infinite possibilities and creativity without end. It is thought of as inspiring and motivating to associate the space where you work with such concepts. Practicing modern minimalism, however, shows how building a space suited to focus rather than chaos helps achieve the dreams and possibilities. It's often said that the most creative people have messy desks and workspaces. Assigning that kind of clutter to every person in search of creativity is like assigning a 4-hour sleep schedule to everyone because that's how Martha Stewart or Jeff Bezos function. Practicing minimalism in your office helps you tap into the creativity by putting down the minimalist organizing methods as a foundation.

In practice, less choice begins with a mental shift when it comes to your work. It's easy to be overwhelmed by the tasks and priorities stacking up in your inbox as well as your mind. Make the choice to focus on what you can control in order to foster productivity. You control how you approach your work and the pattern you follow to complete it. Take a look outside of your work, as well. Identify areas where you can simplify your choices in order to avoid spending time deciding on something. Your home is one place and the work you're doing by reading and applying the principles in this book will lighten the load of choice. Even the simple act of downsizing the amount of cookware in you kitchen creates a few less choices when you open up the cabinet doors.

Even decisions like what to eat and drink are choices drawing on your brain power. Find the routines that take having to decide out of the equation. Find your favorite coffee or tea and stick with that. Plan out your meals for the week concentrating your decision making to one block of time instead of 3 blocks of time every day (plus snacks!). Even your closet is full of decisions to be made. A work uniform would help minimize choice in this area of your life. There's a reason famous CEO's and even regular people who are extremely busy choose to wear the same clothing or same category of clothing each day. They're minimizing choice in the face of all the other important decisions they need to make. Give yourself that same respect.

I encourage streamlining the daily decisions you have to make, but I am not advocating a vanilla lifestyle. Keep your going out dresses and your favorite seasonal drink on deck. You'll need them on the days you set aside for yourself to just focus on you and your family. Taking time away from work is just as important as taking time *to* work. Give yourself space on specific days, to minimize time spent deciding when to have those days to yourself each week. There will be days when the amount of work you've been putting in is wearing on you. Recognize when you're in that phase of work and do what you can to take a mental health day. A spontaneous break from the grind where your decision making is focused on getting a manicure or a massage. Work decisions are not to be made on this day.

Less Tools

I'm going to say something that almost every productivity blog, article, and book out there refuses to admit: forget tools, focus on the work. Forget the best messaging app for small teams, large teams, and in between teams. Forget the best time tracking system or the best timing method to help you focus. Forget the best email suite for communication, the newest laptop, or the latest and greatest phone. In the process of acquiring, learning, and integrating all of these tools, you lose time and energy that could have been devoted to work.

I've tried everything out there to manage projects, communicate with my team, and help me focus on my work. I always come back to simple pen and paper. A written to-do list has always provided a simple way to keep track of tasks and log information needed to keep team members up to date. Combined with a calendar, it's been a boon to productivity and is simple enough to keep me focused on work, not updating a Gantt chart. The problem with the many available productivity hacks is that they require a sort of start up period wherein you're taking time that could be devoted to work and spending it on integrating your style of work into this one box. New hacks are constantly appearing garnering attention and making you question if that would be a better system than what you use now. Productivity hacks will always stay one step ahead of your current system. By relying so much on a productivity tool, you'll be drawn in to whatever bigger and better system comes along.

The same logic applies to technology that is meant to make our work lives better and increase productivity. Sleek advertisements for the latest laptop spark dreams of increased productivity and even better work delivered. But only if you buy it. Your own success can fuel the desire to upgrade your work technology because you deserve it. But be careful. Like productivity hacks, work technology will always stay one step ahead of you. There's always a new version of a laptop or phone on the horizon. You can never really stay on top of it unless you're constantly thinking and deciding on the newest technology to acquire. Don't waste your precious time and mental energy on something that will provide minimal returns at best. With proper maintenance and software upgrades, computers and phones can last longer and provide you with everything you need to do your job well. Don't crowd your mind with anything frivolous. Keep what you have and utilize it to suit your needs. It ultimately saves you money and prevents you from spending your mental energy on something unworthy.

Less Friction

This section could also be called "Less Interruptions" because it is all about minimizing those tiny distractions that pull our brains out of the work. A study from the University of California Irvine followed workers on the job to measure distractions and the impact on their work. What they found is that it takes an average of 23 minutes and 15 seconds to get back on task after a distraction. Multiply that by even a few distractions a day and you're already approaching an hour of work lost each day. An unexpected phone call, a delivery person at your door, or your dog getting into trouble in the house are just a few distractions taking you away from a task.

After that, there's the dozens of notifications received on your phone and desktop pop ups. Each one refocuses your brain, even if it's just information to process and not send a response.

In your office, it's crucial to confront the friction that makes working more difficult.

Remove the desktop pop ups that are often installed when a web page asks you to enable them. Social media sites and email suites are notorious for these pop ups, but your favorite news site is also a source of constant contact. Keep only the tabs and windows open needed to complete the current task. When you're finished with one task, reassess what's open and adjust to set yourself up for the next item on your to-do list.

For your phone, remove email and social media apps completely. Save yourself from the notifications and the irresistible urge to scroll through your feeds. I urge you to try this for one week and see how you do. You'll more than likely find that you missed out on nothing important by keeping these apps off your phone and thus out of your work. If you try it and can't find satisfaction in their absence, there is another option. Go into the settings of each app that sends you notifications. For each one, turn off the notifications. In doing so, you're removing the initial distraction, the ping or vibration of your phone. This allows you to make a conscious choice during intentional breaks to check the apps and review the information you need to know in your email.

Intentional breaks are a crucial part of your workflow. They are the parts of your workday that open your mind and allow it to breathe. Clearing your mind on a walk or scheduled time to take your dog outside to relieve themselves is just as important as buckling down and getting through a task. Take a few minutes and listen to a new album you're excited about. Close your eyes and meditate for 15 or 20 minutes. Refill your water and hydrate. Make yourself a snack and savor it as you eat.

Take a step outside of work so you can return with a clear mind and ready to focus on the next task.

At the beginning of this section I took every productivity hack to task. I wanted you to get your mind off of those disruptive "hacks" and onto your actual work. In doing so, you can start to build a simple system that helps you stay organized. I advocate for a to-do list. The best and simplest way to organize it is by week. The likelihood that you will finish a to-do list made for a specific day is very low. Save yourself some time by dedicating one block of time each week to make a list of tasks that need to be done at some point in the week. With less distractions from other sources, your brain will help you decide what is a priority. Spreading it out over the course of the week not only saves you from spending time every day on a list, but helps you feel more accomplished. It can be disheartening to have to carry something over day after day. In this situation, it is also easy to forget your triumphs.

> <u>A quick note about project management apps</u>:
>
> Your organization is likely to use some manner of project management software to help keep teams informed on departmental and cross-departmental projects. You will need to participate, but not to the point where you spend all your time on it. Keep your simple to-do list. Include the task of updating projects on it so your team knows where you stand with the piece of the puzzle assigned to you.

The first part of this chapter got you out of your head and into a new understanding of your office space. The second part will take you through the practical tips to apply when organizing the office space in your home. If you don't work from home or have a side job that you run from a home office space, take these tips with you wherever you work. You may not be able to choose your furniture style or control all the lighting choices, but applying what you can will have a positive impact on your work. I've put together 5 steps to organizing a home office to fulfill your minimalist dreams.

Step 1: Get Rid Of The Clutter

Every time I step into an office supplies store I am taken by the shiny new desk organizers and tools. Matching staplers and pencil cups are (almost) irresistible. They are also unnecessary. In a modern home office, you need much less in the way of physical supplies than you ever did. A whole cup of pens, pencils, and highlighters are unnecessary. Keeping one pen or pencil at hand is enough for your writing needs. Staplers, three-hole punches, and tape dispensers are also just more clutter that most home offices don't need.

Start with the desktop and find the pieces that you don't use. It may seem as though everything is necessary in an office because there is a cultural idea of what encompasses a proper desk. The matching desk accessories at office supply stores are proof of that theory. Forget what is standard fare for a desktop and think about your work. Most work is conducted over the computer and bypasses paper. This in turn cuts the need for paperclips, staples, tape, highlighters, and more.

Move onto the drawers and get rid of anything you don't use on a daily basis. The unused sticky notes and notepads can be recycled. When you need a new notebook or pad of paper for to-do lists, buy one (and only one). The ruler you've had since college, the scientific calculator from the same era, the broken label maker. These should all go. It's easy to carry so much in the way of office supplies because you place a value on it providing you value in the future. Modern minimalism isn't about finding solutions to your future, it's about giving you the space to focus on the now and be ready for what's to come.

Comb through your shelves and bookcases to find the books, notebooks, and binders that are no longer needed. For books, unless you reference the information on a daily or weekly basis, they are not supporting you anymore. If you need a specific book again in the future, you can find it in an electronic version (often cheaper) or through digital rental from your local library (the cheapest). For old notebooks filled with thoughts, ideas, and work notes, decide what is still useful. If you need information to put together a portfolio, create a project for yourself and follow through. Once you've gleaned the information you need from the notebooks, discard them. Keep recent notebooks that you may need to reference in performance reviews and team meetings. If you're keeping work information in binders, periodically go through and see what is still relevant. Consider a more minimalist storage solution for these papers if you are not accessing them on a daily or weekly basis. A paper box in a neutral color or hanging file storage container with a lid also in a neutral color are two good options.

Your home office is the most likely place to keep papers like passports, birth certificates, mortgage papers, and tax info. Here's the best way to store what you should keep. The most sensitive documents, like wills and birth certificates should be in a safe. Any paperwork related to debt such as mortgage origination documents should be kept until the debt is paid off. Tax papers need to be kept for 7 years, an IRS standard. They can be stored in hanging files to make the best use of container space. Seek out a neutral color and matching file storage boxes to keep the look in line with minimalism.

Papers like statements, receipts, or bills that you can get online should not be kept. Set up paperless statements and billing with your bank as well as your credit card company. Manuals to appliances or other consumer purchases are often easily found online allowing you to get rid of the paper versions. Digitize as much as you can, scan papers into your computer and sort them into folders. Take pictures of the documents in your safe to have a backup version. Pictures are not a complete replacement for a document, but may help in your quest to get one reissued.

Step 2: Make Room For Your Space

If your home office is where you conduct the majority of your work, don't skimp on the location in your home. A room or space with lots of natural light keeps you inspired throughout the day and gives you the opportunity for the sun to tell you the (general) time. Whether you have a room with a door to close or a section of an open room to call your office, define it and distinguish it from the rest of your home. Coordinate the color of your desk with the shelving you use to keep essential work tools. Use an area rug to mark the space and bring textured warmth.

By defining your home office with design or architecture, you're preventing the space from becoming cluttered with other uses. It can make sense to use a space big enough for more than one purpose. However, you don't want your office to become a magnet for everything that doesn't have a defined space. Keep your yoga mats and craft supplies somewhere else. You can consider how the space might be made for more than one purpose, but start with the office first. Then you can move on to integrating other needs into the space using minimalist storage and proper placement of furniture.

Step 3: Make A System For Paper

Paper finds its way into our lives on a daily basis. You might need to print something to work on physically. Walking to the mailbox each day brings in half a dozen or more pieces of paper. Make a system to deal with incoming paper to avoid repeating the step of decluttering on a more regular basis. The first action you can take is writing or emailing to the companies and organizations that send you mail. If its credit card offers or charity fundraisers that you give to no matter how much paper they send, reach out and ask to be taken off their list. This will significantly cut down the flow of paper from your mailbox to your desk.

Second, invest in a small minimal paper shredder to keep by your desk. A shredder will keep your work flowing by taking in even nonsensitive papers and collating the shreds into one bin of recycling. If a shredder is too much space, opt for a small profile recycling bin so you can easily recycle papers without having to leave your office.

Third, file important papers immediately. If you're completely converted to digital, scan it in using a scanner or even better, your phone. There are plenty of apps available for free that will take your digital image and convert it into a document to save.

Step 4: Get Rid Of The Extra

Take on the extra decor and furniture in the room to open the space and give it a clean feel. Diplomas, fancy business card holders, awards, and other office decor items should be stored out of sight or removed from the house. Clear shelves and bookcases of these items to leave space next to the books and storage boxes you've put together.

Clear the walls of anything that's distracting. Keep only what is helpful, such as a mirror to check yourself before a video call or a framed print of a quote that keeps you motivated. Even too many good things can be distracting. Be discerning in what you place on your walls and keep in mind the positive effects that open space has on your brain. You want to keep your mind clear while you work and clean walls support that goal.

Assess the furniture in the space and get rid of anything that doesn't belong in an office or is not helpful for getting your work done. This means goodbye to the hand-me-down easy chair that begs to be napped in everyday around 2:00 p.m. Move this furniture to a better place in your home or get rid of it altogether.

Step 5: Set Up Your Desktop

With all the effort put into removing items that don't support your work, the last thing you want to do is counteract that with a messy desktop. Set ground rules for what can be on your desk at any given time. The most important rule to adopt is only keep items on your desk that you are currently using to work. This is not a place to store things and should not be treated as such. Your efforts to clean out drawers and shelves now present an opportunity to store items that are used on a rotational basis. If you don't have drawers, utilize shelves and minimal storage containers to keep these items.

If your work requires you to oscillate between computer tasks and paper tasks that take up the entire desktop, consider how to maximize surface area. Find a drawer to keep your laptop, keyboard, and mouse when not in use. If you have a desktop computer, invest in monitor stands that affix them to the wall. This leaves usable space underneath and allows you to set the monitor at eye level for comfort throughout the day.

Keeping the top of your desk clean is an ongoing effort. You should aim to deal with whatever lands on your desk when you receive it. That may not always be possible. In cases like these, it's helpful to designate a drawer or box on your desk to catch the things that pile up. Be sure to sort through it on a regular basis to keep it from getting out of hand.

A modern minimalist home office is not just about continuing the practice of minimalism in another room of your home. It is a crucial application that supports your mental well-being by supporting your work. It facilitates productivity with simplicity, reduced distraction, and a clean environment. Your minimalist home office is a supporter of professional growth and a gain in mental clarity. Refer back to this chapter often. Work is not a static state but one of constant changes. Keep rooted in the principles and steps laid out in this chapter to support yourself long term.

Chapter 8. Minimalist Storage

The Secrets to Joy in Efficiency

Clothes Closet - Love Everything You See

Your clothes closet may be intended just for clothing, but they're often taken up by other clutter as well. Couple that with how quickly new clothes can pile up on hangers and you're facing a closet disaster. You can never find your favorite top, items become buried for months in the chaos, and you dread putting clean clothes away. The goal of a minimalist closet is to prevent all of the above. It's about decluttering, but also about how you organize what you keep and what steps are needed to support a calm minimalist space. This chapter is for every closet. You may have a grand walk-in closet with high ceilings or an alcove with a door and a hanging rod. Many people live with just a freestanding armoire or similar clothes-hanging furniture piece. Your closet may be unique, but practicing modern minimalism in this space of your home is universal. Combined with the buying and shopping habits in the second chapter, the following steps give you a closet you love to open every morning.

Find Low-Hanging Fruit: Damaged Clothing

The items that are no longer in wearable condition provide an easy entry point into organizing your entire closet. They're low hanging fruit because they are no longer functional. They're objectively unwearable and don't necessarily have the same emotional effect on you as the top you bought last week or your grandmother's wedding dress.

I put this step first so you can practice going through your closet with an easy search filter. File through all your clothing and pick out each one that is stained, ripped, faded, or broken. You're likely to have a good idea of these pieces before you start, so this step will go quickly. By removing these pieces, you also begin to open up space in your closet for the next steps in organizing.

Mid-Hanging Fruit: Clothes That Don't Fit

This step is only slightly more difficult, but easier to tackle after completing the first step. Get rid of the clothes that don't fit. You may have tried on a piece at the store and found when you got home it just doesn't fit correctly. There are pieces that are too big or too small that you thought could work anyway. There are pieces that fit but were never really your style and have stayed on the hanger since you brought them home. Whatever the case, they are weighing on you and need to be gone.

In addition to taking up space in your closet, they're taking up space in your mind each time you see them in the closet and wonder why it is you can't wear them. They can spark questions of "Why can't I pull that off?" or "If only I could lose/gain 10 pounds." These thoughts and questions are part of what modern minimalism is working against. This mental clutter is draining and unsupportive of a meditative peaceful life. Your home should be a safe place and by removing triggers of negative thoughts you can support that goal. Save your mental space for more important things. Take comfort knowing the clothes that you take from your closet can be given away to benefit someone else.

Buck the Trends

As you're going through your closet, you're apt to find pieces bought based on trend and less on enduring quality and style. Reassess retaining trendy pieces in your closet to avoid ending up with out-of-style clothing when the next trend sweeps in. Remember to take a minute to understand how these trends end up in your closet. The fashion industry, and especially fast-fashion retailers, constantly change the course of style to keep consumers coming back. If they all just focused on classic styles with quality materials, consumers wouldn't need to buy as many clothes as often.

Knowing that, take time to look at the clothing you do have and the favorite pieces that spend very little time on a hanger. Start to put together your own style and look. Find the pieces that go together well and make you feel wonderfully confident. Lean into it and build what you have in your closet around that look. In addition to the positivity radiating from confidence in your wardrobe, you can shop for new pieces knowing exactly the style you need.

Store Seasonal Clothes Elsewhere

There are professional organizers who would encourage you to keep all your clothes together in the same closet. They argue that seeing everything you have provides the mental reminder that you have enough and lessens the temptation to shop. I disagree with that idea because if you're practicing modern minimalism, you're already avoiding unnecessary shopping and have created storage solutions that prevent forgetting what you have. A clothes closet with open space around the in-season pieces positively impacts your mind. On the contrary, a full closet with every piece of clothing you own stuffed onto racks and into bins ignites stress.

Take your seasonal clothes and store them in labeled containers in a separate closet or on the highest shelves of your clothes closet. It's up to you to decide if you want clear or opaque containers. However, with proper labeling including a list of each item, you can create even cleaner lines in your closet with opaque containers.

In order to keep your seasonal items in the best shape, assess the threats from climate and bugs. If you live in a humid climate, invest in products that draw moisture out of the air. Keep these in the closet with the stored clothing items to prevent smells and mildew. Almost any climate is subject to moths and depending on where you store your seasonal items in your house, the threat may be higher. Cedar wood is excellent at repelling moths naturally. Cedar chests were popular for a reason. You can find cedar chips or finished balls at most home stores. They can be easily stored with your clothes in their containers.

Avoid the Diderot Effect

The Diderot Effect came from 18th century French philosopher Denis Diderot. He sought to explain the cause of overconsumption. He put forth the idea that if a consumer purchases one item, it can quickly spiral into more purchases and overconsumption. The Diderot Effect happens in every category of purchase, but it can easily ramp up when it comes to your closet. A gorgeous dress in a boutique window display calls you and before you know it, new shoes and a purse join it on the sales counter. You needed the shoes because nothing else you own matches and the purse was with the display begging to not be separated from the dress.

Find the byproducts of this phenomenon in your closet and get rid of them. In the future, keep in mind the pieces you already own and only add new pieces that fit in. Getting your closet to the point where you can easily see what you have will support this habit.

Keep One, Get Rid of the Rest

Everyone has duplicate clothing items in their closet. These pieces may vary slightly by color or style, but their function is the same. Look closely at what you have and decide how many you truly need. A sweater for every day of the week is too much for someone living in a climate that stays warm most of the year. You only need one pair of running shoes and to buy new ones when those wear out. Multiple winter jackets take up a lot of space and each require a cleaning at the end of the season. Find one in your closet that's a neutral color and wear it season after season.

The idea is to love everything you have in your closet. When you stock up on pieces with the same function, you inevitably end up with one you wear most often. Imagine making your closet into a space where you only have the items you wear all the time. Think about how much more satisfying it is to open the door and see only the items you love most. Keep that in mind as you go through and remove duplicate items from the space.

Physically Hold Each Item

It can be easy to rush through organizing your closet, especially as you get further into it and begin to question if there's a machine spitting out clothes behind your back. Don't let yourself rush this process. It's important to handle each item individually and assess its value in your closet. In doing so, you're allowing your mind the ability to process why you're keeping or getting rid of an item. Holding your favorite sweater from college will allow you to soak in the memories it triggers while also realizing the pilling is out of control and should be donated.

Give yourself that space to process the pieces in your closet. If it seems overwhelming to take on an entire closet at once, cut it into doses. Start with all your shoes, then all your dresses, then your jackets, and continue through the categories. Break it up to make the process easier and to allow you to look back on it with pride.

Keep Testing

If you still struggle to contain your clothes, try a different approach before diving into some of the steps above. Select about half the pieces in your wardrobe and put them away for one week (two if you can stand it!). During the week, dress yourself with what's left in your closet and note how many times you remember a particular piece that was stored away. You'll find that at the end of the period, most of the clothing hidden away did not cross your mind and its function was fulfilled by another piece.

If you found that to be the case, dive deeper into your wardrobe with some of the previous steps. The test shows how you can easily live with less and the steps laid out in this first section of the chapter show you just how to do it.

The intention of a minimalist closet is not to ration clothing like a scarce good, but to assemble the pieces you truly love. They are to be enjoyed and easily accessible in one place. In doing so, you're creating an aesthetically pleasing space that functions beautifully each day.

Garage or Storage Closet - Store With Intention

Everyone has a catch-all storage space in their home. If you're in a house, townhome, or condo that usually looks like a garage. For most apartments and condos, that looks like a storage closet sometimes within or just outside of the unit. Whatever it looks like for you, it is often the most overlooked space for practicing modern minimalism. However, if it is looked at as the one place minimalism doesn't apply it can fill up quickly with items from other rooms.

Start by finding your intentions for the space. Is it simply to store holiday decorations, out of season clothes, and your trusty tennis racket? Do you handle your own lawn maintenance and require a set of tools to get it done? Ask yourself what the space is to be used for and organize around that purpose (or set of purposes). A garage or storage closet should never be a place to keep things out of sight and thus out of mind. It has a purpose like every other room in your home.

Clear Out Your Space

Assess what you use your garage or storage space for and use that as your guide in clearing the clutter. If you are a home DIY guru, organize your supplies and get rid of old ones. If you haven't touched the golf clubs sitting in the corner since high school, donate them. Go through the stacked bins of holiday decorations and discard anything that is no longer functional. If you have duplicates of tools, pick the highest quality tool to keep. Get rid of the rest. Make sure to take into account other items from your home that will be stored in this space seasonally. Account for the space those items will need when organizing other items.

If you've been in your home for more than a year and there are unopened boxes in your garage or storage closet, they're most likely unnecessary. Go through the contents and get rid of the items no longer contributing to your life. Remember your purpose for the space and don't let clutter get in the way.

Vehicle Storage

One item that is often overlooked as a piece to get rid of is your vehicle. If you're living in a dense metropolitan area with more than a few transit options, this may be the right minimalist move for you. Freeing up the assigned parking space in your building's garage or opening your private garage can have positive effects on not only your home but your wallet, as well. You may save parking rent each month or find that with a garage cleared, you can convert the space into something more useful (like a guest room). The average car payment in the U.S. reached $554 a month in the first quarter of 2019.

When you weigh the costs and hassle of car ownership (insurance, parking fees, traffic tickets, maintenance) with adopting transit you might find car-free is the way to go. Consider the alternative modes of transportation which in major metropolitan areas now include scooters, bikeshares, buses, light-rail, trains, walkable neighborhoods, and even convenient cars for rent on most blocks. Start by replacing one trip a week with these alternatives and see how it fits into your lifestyle. A car-free lifestyle supports minimalism by giving you one less job to do throughout your day. Instead of avoiding fender benders on your way to work, you can enjoy a podcast or book on your bus commute. Getting out of the hassles associated with car ownership also supports calm and peacefulness in yet another aspect of your home life.

Store Everything Off The Floor

In garages and storage closets, piles of items are often the closest to organization you find. In both instances, valuable floor space is used up making it difficult to access everything when you need it. A garage that requires you to dig through and move things piled on the floor is not functional. Even more than that, it's stressful. Considering the work you have to put in just to get to the bins of holiday decorations can make you avoid the task at all costs.

Make organization easier in the space by committing to storing everything somewhere other than the floor. Invest in cabinetry or other storage that allows you to store, tools, bins, and other items together. Consider the categories of items you've pared down to in the previous step and work out the logical storage layout. Power tools should definitely go together, but they should also be close to project materials that require them.

Find The Right Hierarchy of Storage

When you're putting together your storage system, take into consideration which items need to be the most accessible and which ones are used less often. Holiday decorations, seasonal clothes, specific tools, and other items should be stored up high. In doing so, you're creating easy access to the items you use more regularly. You're also creating a minimalist aesthetic that allows you to associate calm and peacefulness with the space. Be sure to label containers, even if they're behind cabinet doors. This will make it easy to identify what you have and where it is kept.

Carefully consider items that you've kept in the garage or storage closet to see if they should be stored elsewhere in your home. You might have seasonal items that should be stored in another closet or the attic where they would be closer to their final use. It's easy to overestimate the amount of space in a garage because they're so large and open. Approach it like you would any other room in your home. You will need to account for the space taken up by stored items, along with the space needed to conduct activities associated with the area.

The work you put into the other rooms in your home is supported when you take the time to declutter and organize your garage. By avoiding the usual pitfalls of using the garage space as a dumping ground for items you can't find a spot for elsewhere, you support your minimalist efforts in the rest of your home. By tackling both your closet and your garage in this chapter, the practice of modern minimalism in your home comes full circle. Remember to take these rooms one step at a time and give yourself the mental space to process every item you encounter.

Chapter 9. Minimalist Exterior

A Look You Never Thought Possible

Your front yard or balcony of your apartment is the first part of your home to greet you. Applying the principles of modern minimalism to this space supports the work you've done in the rest of your home. A minimalist yard is low-maintenance, potentially without a need to mow or water grass. It takes into account your climate and region with touches of the best native plants. Different textures come together to create an aesthetic that suits your unique terrain and home style. Practicing minimalism in your front yard brings together the calming feeling of open space with your unique style.

Your backyard is often a sanctuary in nature providing an escape from the indoors during warm weather months. It may also support you by growing food for consumption. It's visible from most rooms in the home and often that includes your bedroom. Its design should immediately disarm and put at ease anyone who steps out into it. There are features in both the front and backyard that will turn these spaces into a beautiful minimalist landscape. In the first part of this chapter, I'll share the features that distinguish a minimalist front yard and in the latter half provide tips to creating your dream minimalist backyard.

The Front Yard - A Calming Welcome Home

Curb appeal is an important aesthetic of any home. For your minimalist front yard, your goal should be to harness the current landscape to create curb appeal that is not only aesthetically pleasing, but evokes calm and peacefulness. As a gateway into the rest of your home, it's important to carefully assess your front yard and make the right changes. Below are the features that taken separately and together achieve the goal of a modern minimalist yard.

Feature 1: Native Plants

One of the outcomes of increased mobility over the last century and a half is the spread of plants to many different parts of the country and even the world. Plants that take off in areas where they are not native are considered an invasive species. Depending on the plant and its viability, it can distress the native plant life and create an imbalance in native wildlife dependent on those plants. A minimalist front yard will incorporate only native plants for the invasive species argument above as well as other important factors.

Native species thrive in their homes because of their ability to evolve and adapt to the conditions present. They're stronger as a result and can stand up to the climate in your region better than other plants. The market for native plants is strong making it easy to find experts in your area who not only sell native plants but offer knowledge and expertise. Take advantage of local independently owned greenhouses and landscape centers who can help you find the plants to fit your yard.

Be judicious with your selection of plants as it can be easy to overwhelm the softscape sections of your lawn. The softscape sections are the areas where plant life and softer elements reign. For each section, start small in your selection of plants to keep maintenance down and create space between each plant. A common feature of minimalist yards is the boxwood shrub. They're hearty and easily shaped to create clean lines as well as space between each one. Boxwoods have grown in popularity over time to the point where many different varieties have been bred to withstand a number of different climates. Refer back to the landscape experts at your local retailer to learn if there is a species of boxwood that's suited to your region and can live in harmony with native plants.

Feature 2: Limited Color Palette

This feature applies to both the plants and the architectural elements you bring into your yard. It's easy to clutter up your landscape design with the many variations of color available for purchase. Whether its plants or pavers, color can crowd your yard and take away the mental calm that comes from a streamlined design. One way to avoid falling into an endless bouquet of color is to plan out your yard in advance. Select the plants and types of textured features you are going to use beforehand.

There are professional landscape architects who specialize in planning the yard. If you choose not to hire a professional, you can still plan out what you need. Start from the perimeter of your home and work your way out. Consider the heights of your windows, the architecture of your porch, and the placement of your walkway as well as your driveway. Spend time measuring the size of the softscape areas so you can calculate the space needed between plants and thus how many fit in each area.

By taking this critical time to plan, you can identify not only how many of each feature you need, but the colors you'll be using. In this planning process, you can identify the colors you want and choose plants based on that palette. To keep the most minimal look, find only plants in the green color family. You can complement them with hard features such as stones, boulders, or pavers in a nude or tan color family.

Feature 3: Hardscapes

I've mentioned hard elements such as rocks or boulders a few times already. These elements provide a contrast to the softer ones and often stand on their own as a feature. In addition to things like rocks or pavers, hardscapes include elements such as walkways, driveways, patios, decks, and fencing. You may choose a yard that features hardscapes exclusively or integrate them with softscapes for a unique look. However you assemble your yard, take note of the variations in hardscape elements.

For a large yard, concrete provides a simple and effective look with easy maintenance. You can choose colored concrete in shades such as dark brown or a nude shade of tan. Concrete works best in driveways and walkways. For patios in large yards, consider paver bricks that can be assembled in clean line patterns. Crushed rock and gravel can also work in large yards to create a hardscape area that's aesthetically appealing and minimalist.

For a smaller yard, you'll have less maintenance and can get creative with crushed rock and gravel. You can use gravel in your driveway and then pavers in your walkway. A smaller yard can sustain concrete just as well as a larger yard, but don't be afraid to use other products to create hardscapes. Whatever you choose, make sure it balances well with the softscapes you use or the other hardscapes.

I mentioned fences and want to elaborate on their purpose in a front yard. They can create a more intentional feature when used against a blank wall of your home or serve a purpose as a perimeter feature. Horizontal slats in wooden fences create clean lines and pleasing visuals. You can also use metal in a neutral color, like black or brown, to add a different element to your yard.

Feature 4: Simple Furniture

Outdoor furniture has become elaborate in design over the last several years. Outdoor rugs the size of indoor area rugs have taken off as a must-have for your outdoor space. Furniture often requires cushions and is sold with throw pillows. The concept of bringing the indoors outside when it comes to comfort and features is admirable. However, it increases the maintenance if you have an area rug inside that needs to be cleaned as well as one outside. If you're stuck cleaning cushion covers and throw pillows of the dust from outside, the benefits they promise are cancelled out.

Furniture in your front yard should be sparse and intentionally selected for its function. Woods like teak and acacia provide the neutral colors needed to blend in with any style. Teak also stands up better to the elements providing style and functionality for years to come. Avoid a lot of clashing colors of the furniture and any accessories you may have. Choose simple, but comfortable, cushions if you require them. Consider how the furniture will complement the style of the yard and also provide functionality. If you have a wraparound porch, consider a separate seating area and adorning the other sections of the porch with simple neutral colored pottery. Be sure to leave space between each element (furniture and décor) to keep with the minimalist look.

Feature 5: Little to No Ornaments

Rather than clutter your yard with craft fair finds and mismatched birdbaths, choose only the best ornaments for your yard and get rid of the rest. Assess the best place in your yard for the pieces you keep and consider functionality in your decision to keep an item. A proper birdbath will invite more nature into the space while providing a complementary ornament that's pleasing to the eye. A neutral color container, like a vintage barrel, can provide visual appeal while also storing rainwater to be used for irrigation.

Making do with less ornamentation is not about clearing the yard of visual interest, but instead drawing the eye to the yard as a whole. Using neutral colors, clean lines, and sparse ornaments your attention is focused on the whole picture. If you have too many grabbing colors represented by too many objects, your mind jumps from one to another. Your yard should have an aesthetically pleasing and calming effect, not the opposite.

Feature 6: Grass-Free Zones

A minimalist yard should include minimal maintenance. The practice embraces native plants and simple furniture to support the low-maintenance label. Your front yard design can support this with either a grass-free yard or zones where hardscapes replace grass. You will need to consider city, county, or Homeowners Association rules about grass ratios. Once you have the requirements, take full advantage of those guidelines to minimize time spent maintaining your yard.

Grass that is not native to an area requires mowing, fertilization, weed control, and irrigation. Mowing may not take very long and is less frequent in dryer months, but the rest of the work to keep it green is enormous. Take back as much time as you can by cutting down on the square footage of grass. Alternatives to grass include hardscape features like rocks, planting native vines or other ground coverings, and even seeding native wildflowers. Wildflowers in particular are hardy and can grow within their native climate without much care. If you must have grass, whether through regulation or your desired aesthetic, find native grasses that thrive in your region. That will cut down on some of the maintenance associated with the typical specialty non-native grasses found in most yards.

Feature 7: A Water Feature

Your yard is the best representation of the earth element, so why not add in the water element as well? The sound of water is calming and would be a welcome sensory stimulation upon returning home after your day. For a front yard, consider open wall space to create a cascading feature that is the focal point. A simple fountain with clean lines can also stand alone in the midst of a hardscape foundation. A section of rocks with a concrete pad in the middle supporting a fountain is striking and achieves the desired effect. A backyard is also worthy of a water feature, but more on that in the next section.

Consider your front yard the first room in your home. It is the foyer through which you enter into the rest of your space. Treat it as such by taking your practice of minimalism to it and giving it the attention it deserves. Incorporating the above features based on the topographical, regional, and regulatory characteristics will give you the minimalist yard to match the rest of your home. Each feature can be adapted to the size and specifications of your yard. Even balconies and patios of apartments or condos can utilize some of the features above. As with every other room in your home, you need to assess your needs and what is feasible for you. Don't neglect this area of your home, build time to give it proper attention, starting with the simple act of decluttering.

The Backyard - A Garden To Remember

With the front yard sharing your style with the rest of the world, your backyard is a sanctuary in which you can retreat from the outside world. It should flow seamlessly from the sanctuary that is the inside of your home. It's a place to grow food for you and your family. A place to enjoy good weather. It helps balance your time spent indoors by inviting you to retreat into nature. Consider you and your family's needs as far an outdoor space and then plan from there. Like your front yard, your backyard should support your needs while also demanding the least amount of effort in the form of maintenance and upkeep. Landscape designer Julie Farris, based in New York, said it best: "Looking at your garden should not make you think of your to-do list." That statement is powerful and the goal to keep in mind as you plan your backyard.

Feature 1: Each Space Is Defined

In small and large yards alike, defining space positively impacts not only the aesthetic but the feeling of the yard. Define each space using materials that either match or contrast with the surrounding landscape. You may use pavers to define the space around a pool or other water feature. A wooden fence section can be used to support climbing plants and provide privacy. Bricks can be used to create raised beds delineating the plants from the hard or softscape feature that surrounds it. The concept of a raised bed has the space separation built in, you just need to choose the materials.

When defining the yard as a whole, consider the different materials that can be used to create privacy. Perhaps you want a green privacy feature using hardy native plants that grow quickly or can be purchased already mature. Wooden fences can be built and stained to match the color palette chosen for the backyard.

Feature 2: Privacy Abounds

I briefly touched on privacy when offering options for separating space, but the feature warrants its own section. Backyards are by their very name associated with privacy. Your home and land is situated to put the front yard as the face of the property leaving the backyard a bit of a mystery. Sometimes privacy is provided naturally by a nature preserve backing up to the property. It can also be provided by the geography of the rural region you reside. Oftentimes, you need to add your own privacy. It's an important feature to have no matter how it's created because a backyard's purpose is to provide a retreat.

Depending on your yard and the proximity of neighbors, you may only be able to provide privacy to one section of your yard. In order to do so, select the space that would provide the most benefit if privatized. It may be the patio just off the back door or a sanctuary between a few established trees beyond the house. After finding the space, consider the materials needed to create seclusion. If it is a screen porch connected to the house, consider utilizing a horizontal wooden fence for plants to climb. You can also install planters in an appealing pattern. Each fence section can stand independently allowing breezes to enter the porch while keeping visibility into the space to a minimum.

For a space in the yard not connected to the house, consider evergreens that can grow up around a thoughtfully arranged seating area. Using greenery versus another material helps camouflage your sanctuary space and keep it private. Evergreens would also work wonderful for spaces connected to the house if you're trying to keep the green color for continuity.

Feature 3: Hardscape Foundations

Hardscapes are just as important in the backyard as they are in the front yard. They often have even more impact because they take your focus off maintaining greenery and allow use of your backyard to the fullest extent.

If you're facing a large yard with a lot of greenery to maintain, consider starting at the exit to the house and let a hardscape feature ripple out covering more ground. If you have a deck off your house, start with laying a medium-sized rock or gravel around the perimeter. In the next ring, use small stone, and in the outer ring, use poured concrete. By laying the hardscape materials and extending the footprint of the deck, you are dedicating more space to a maintenance-free yard. This method can also be used for concrete patios or paver patios that extend off your home. I highlight this hardscape design specifically because it supports the goal for a backyard to flow seamlessly from the home.

Feature 4: Simple Designs

A helpful thought exercise is to look at your garden through the lens of Japanese garden philosophy. Imagine your yard as nature in miniature. Rather than an entire forest, you're planting a few trees. Instead of fields of wild grass, you've created sections where it can thrive in harmony with surrounding hardscape features.

The easiest way to keep it simple is define your neutral color palette before you start selecting features. Then, consider the needs of you and your family to define the purposes your yard will need to fulfill. The larger the yard, the more uses you can harness without stacking features on top of each other. "Simple" can seem like a loose term when you begin to consider the needs of a large family. There's no reason why a yard that needs to support kids' sports, dogs' activities, or entertaining regular guests can't be simple. It's all about how you approach it and the space you're given to work with. Rank the needs of your family and plan carefully how to fit them into the yard.

Feature 5: Raised Beds and Planters

Well-designed and made raised beds provide not only visual interest to your backyard but true functionality. Raised beds using bricks or pavers built wide allow for a place to sit while tending the garden. This design also keeps you from bending over for long periods of time while pruning or harvesting.

For the least amount of maintenance, use native plants carefully spaced to provide an appealing visual pattern. If you'd like your garden to support you and your family's food needs, a raised bed can provide easy access to harvests. Space seeds or seedlings carefully and don't overcrowd the bed.

Planters, or containers, can add visual appeal to your yard without requiring the work of clearing and tilling large parts of your yard for planting. You can control the soil without relying on what's naturally occurring in your yard thereby supporting strong healthy plants. Make sure you select containers that fit into a neutral color palette. You can also take advantage of seasons to change up greenery and color throughout the year.

Feature 6: Water Element

Backyards provide the perfect backdrop for large simple water features or small elaborate ones for you to enjoy. A pool is the perfect choice and may already be a part of the landscape depending on your region. In a pool area, it's important to keep pool accessories and toys out of sight. Keep a teak storage container nearby to quickly access anything you need for the pool. Opt for a monochromatic pool foundation color and use pavers or concrete to create a minimalist deck.

Fountains, whether part of a pool set up or standalone, contribute to the feeling of serenity your backyard should evoke. Be sure to keep the mechanical aspects out of sight and consider fountain options that put reservoirs into the ground. By having the fountain reservoirs just below the surface, the transition from yard to fountain is seamless. You can find the materials yourself for a fountain build or consult an expert for an easy to install feature.

Your backyard is part of the natural flow of your home. It should seamlessly blend with your home providing privacy, usefulness, and a sense of calm. Upon entering your backyard, you should feel at ease and see the features as complementary of one another. Each feature in this section contributes to the perfect minimalist backyard. Take time to assess your family's needs, yard size, and materials at hand to create a retreat from daily life right in your home.

There's a reason modern minimalism is often referred to as a practice. It is an ongoing experiment in finding ways to best enhance your life. Rather than achieving an enhanced life by consuming and cluttering your home, modern minimalism uses a specific set of tools to create space in your home that in turn creates space in your mind. Its purpose is not to trade in all your materials for a desolate space, but to sharpen your focus on the things and experiences that matter most. In your practice, you find mental clarity and space that can be reallocated to finding your own highest and best purpose.

Conclusion

You picked up this book because you've attempted minimalism before, have heard about it, or because a large change in your life has brought you to the practice. I count myself as a member of the latter. However you found your way to this book, it's for you. It's not here to promise a quick fix or a solution to everything that's going on in your life. It's here to help you bring minimalism into your home and free up the space in your mind taken up by clutter. By aligning yourself with the objects in your life, you're able to more easily tackle other areas of life.

I put this book together because of how much minimalism has helped me. I've seen firsthand the positive effects of ridding my home of clutter. There's the immediate rush of walking into a clean room the first few times. What surprised me, however, is the lasting impact on my mood from practicing minimalism. In each space, I've organized the items and set up tools that make it easy to keep what I initially set up. Tasks like laundry, dishes, or cleaning no longer feel like "must do" chores but simply routines that provide real benefit. Everything in this book has helped me focus on my own purpose and even deal with the difficult valleys of life. I know it can do the same for you.

Taking each chapter separately, it might seem difficult to envision their ability to align your mind with the objects in your home. Wrapped up together, it becomes clear the ways in which space between clothes hanging in the closet and planters in the backyard combine to give you a neutral space to just *be*.

Dedicating time to each room in your home and setting it up to best support you is the best kind of self-care. You're sacrificing a little time now to open up your future to every possibility. You're ensuring that peace, calm, and serenity remain a part of your lifestyle for years to come.

Each chapter is ordered to maximize your entry or re-entry into the practice of modern minimalism. Each meant to be referenced again and again throughout your practice. While some solutions are meant for specific spaces, there are a few common tools and mindsets to keep with you at all times:

- Clutter is enemy number one to your sanity and your practice. It takes up space in your mind as well as your home.

- Use mechanisms given to stem the flow of clutter and prevent it from piling up. These include rethinking how you shop and what you buy. Your organization in each room will also keep clutter down.

- Be honest about your needs and desires in each room. Not everything in your home is useful or positively contributing to a peaceful mind. Honesty up front means you're less likely to repeat decluttering and organizing in the near future.

- Each space has its purpose and each purpose has its space. Our homes support a variety of needs depending on our lifestyle. Give each important part of your life the space it needs to support you.

- Make space between objects in every room. This simple action has immediate effect, even if you're just beginning your practice.

- If you haven't used something recently, you're not likely to use it again in the near future. Send it on its way knowing that you can get another one if you need it. Maybe someone else could use it.

- If a room or situation overwhelms you, start small. Minimalism is a marathon, not a sprint. You need to get to the end at your own pace.

I want you to end this book feeling like there are options and tools that fit your lifestyle. We do not all live in the same type of dwelling. Size and location as well as renting versus owning will affect how you practice minimalism. The practice is not just for people who can afford an Eichler-designed home in the Bay Area of California. It's for a young grad student living in the middle of a university town. It's for the recent grad who traded more space for a central location in a walkable neighborhood. It's for retirees and families who want to get a handle on the clutter life accumulated. No matter your situation, each chapter has you in mind. Refer back often to the chapters and sections that speak to you and your dwelling.

This book is meant to be picked up again and again. It will travel with you through life and through the stages of your practice. These pages contain the solutions to break down every barrier preventing you from living your life to its fullest purpose. Take with you the powerful knowledge that you are capable and deserving of each and every benefit found in a modern minimalist lifestyle. You're worth the work to find peacefulness, calm, and serenity in every room of your home. You're worthy and capable, no matter what anyone says. You've reached the end of this book, but you're at the beginning of a new chapter in your life. Live it well.

Clean Your House Like A Pro

Proven Methods to Keep Your Home Organized, Deep Clean All Your Rooms and Tidy Up Your House

By

Grace Burke

Introduction

Welcome! If you picked up this book, you've most likely reached a dilemma with your cleaning habits. If you looked up from this introduction and scanned the room you're in, you might see piles of clothes, a collection of fur building up in the corner, and perhaps a layer of grime on your closest window. You mentally take note that the windows need a good cleaning and start to rack your brain for the date you last cleaned them. You may even get up the nerve to clean them all in the morning (if on a Saturday). You spend 3 hours getting them crystal clear and turn around to see the dozens of other surfaces in dire need of attention.

If any of that sounds familiar, you're in the right place. This book is for everyone who dreams of a clean, functional home and has found one roadblock after another trying to get to that point. It's here to take the burdens of housekeeping off you and help you grow to appreciate the routine of cleaning. It takes the guesswork out of the effectiveness of different cleaning products by providing its own set of test results. It gathers the massive bulk of cleaning tasks and breaks them down in a way that returns your weekends to you. More importantly, it's here to eliminate your frustrations over the planning and execution of cleaning tasks so you can focus on more important things in your life.

Before now, you may have felt the only hope your home had for a clean start required gathering your closest friends to help you scrub from top to bottom. It was certainly how I felt when faced with a 3,000 square foot home with several cats, my own full-time job, a ninety minute commute, and a studio-size vacation rental to manage.

I was no stranger to cleaning when I inherited my home and added my lifestyle to it. I have been cleaning houses since high school and had seen everything from abandoned homes with mystery stains on floors to new construction high-rise apartments in need of a simple dusting. I found cleaning others' homes to be soothing and felt they granted me a sense of accomplishment when I finished. I curated my own set of supplies including a treasured vacuum that worked so well, carpets looked brand new. I enjoyed sharing my knowledge of how to clean an antique cast iron tub and what to do with soap scum building up on acrylic shower walls.

I relied on this experience heavily to find my routine in my new home. Like anyone, I craved the fresh start that comes with a completely spotless home. If I was going to find that fresh start, however, I was going to have to confront my schedule. I was knee deep in vacation rental bookings, long days at the office, keeping cats well cared for, and the little bit of time carved out just to breathe. It didn't happen overnight, but I took my house from an allergy bomb to ready for guests at any hour. The difference was extraordinary. I no longer felt like every weekend was dedicated to scrubbing top to bottom to turn over the vacation rental. I found there were nights that I finally had nothing to do in the way of housework and those began to stack up.

I found not only savings in my time after implementing my cleaning method, but a savings in money, too. Every ad on social media for cleaning product delivery services called to me. I had a host of new items and surfaces to keep clean that my old arsenal of products couldn't cover. I had to expand my collection and that meant testing (aka spending money) on new products. Once I found what worked, along with a few homemade alternatives that cost pennies on the dollar, my spending went way down. I was able to clean more surfaces, more often, and for less money.

I also found that the deep cleaning and subsequent maintenance cleaning protected furniture and fixtures from premature aging. I saw this in action when I visited a friend who had installed a vanity sink in their bathroom less than 6 months prior. It wasn't top shelf quality, but I could see how the buildup of dirt around the faucet had actually started eating away at the shiny metallic surface. It hadn't even been a year and the several hundred dollar vanity needed a new faucet! I was tempted in that moment to rush home and check every fixture for signs of deterioration. I restrained, but I could not forget one of the greatest benefits of cleaning-- the money saved on costly repairs, frequent upgrades, and new items that come from neglecting what you currently own.

I'm familiar with my own sense of accomplishment after performing even the most mundane task of loading the dishwasher. But there's actual evidence from studies that show a positive relationship between mental health and a clean home. Originally published in 2008, a UCLA study in the Personality and Social Psychology bulletin looks at 60 dual-income spouses to find whether time spent at home is restful or detracting. What they found is that in homes with unfinished projects or tasks left undone, there were more negative associations with living there. In homes where cleanliness reigned, study participants reported being happier while occupying their home. Even in a small case study like this, those results are powerful. I want that sense of restfulness and relaxation for everyone who reads this book. Not just for the dual-income households who may have hired cleaning services. Anyone can find the serenity that comes from a clean home and this book is here to help.

Now that you've been struck by the fear of decaying faucets and then rapidly uplifted by the benefits of boosted moods, let's get to work. You may have company visiting very soon. You might be dreaming of getting that vacation rental off the ground. You may be preparing yourself for an impending holiday season full of gatherings, gifts, and oh so much to do before then. Don't worry. The best time to start something new is right now. This book is going to bring you step-by-step into a new era for your home. Follow them closely to find the balance you seek. Each chapter of this book is structured for you to refer back whenever you need to refresh your strategy.

Relax, curl up, and let's get started on your journey to a new home.

Chapter 1: The Purpose of a Clean Home

You're here now with this book because you're ready for a change. You want a system of cleaning that you can not only live with, but enjoy. You may have tried your own system or that of another expert with poor results. You may have been skating by with the bare minimum because it's just not something that is taught like math or science. You may even be like I was: married to a routine until illness, an excess of work, or extracurricular activities took all of your free time. Whatever the reason, it is unique to you and your experience. The *importance* of a clean home will also depend on you and your situation. Take a moment now to ask yourself the question "Why is a clean home important to me?" After thinking for a few minutes, write down the top 3 reasons your mind rested on. You might think of more than 3, write those down, too. I'm willing to bet that there is a combination of personal and professional reasons on your list.

In the personal category, you may have written something related to being proud of your home. You're not alone in this. Your home reflects who you are and what makes you unique. You spend a large portion of your income on rent or a mortgage. You spend most of your time outside of work and on other activities in your home. It's where family gathers, pets spend their lives, and memories are made. It's no wonder a clean home is important to you! Your pride is simply a reflection of the many ways in which your home contributes to your life. You may not be in your "dream home" where the current inefficiencies and daily inconveniences are magically solved by new technology (or a better layout). However, listing pride as the reason is proof enough you have exactly what you need to love your home.

You may have also written down the desire for a presentable home whenever company comes calling. You find it important to be ready for guests on short notice. You may also just be tired of cycling through bare minimum everyday cleaning followed by a mad rush deep clean before family visits. Whatever the details, you're ready for the calm peacefulness that comes with a presentable home.

The importance of a clean home also has to do with your profession. A vacation rental lives or dies by reviews with one of the top categories being cleanliness. There are even separate categories in the review process dedicated to highlighting how clean or unclean the space. This isn't a surprise when you consider your own travels and what you rate as necessary for a pleasant hotel stay. You expect not only clean towels and fresh soap, but a fresh floor, pleasant scent, and no sign of previous occupants. Guests in your vacation rental expect the same.

Your professional reason may have more to do with a business you run out of your home. Clients and potential customers may visit on occasion. As they expect a clean environment when entering a commercial office space, they will want the same from your home office. Meeting and exceeding their expectations inspires trust and respect that translates into more work for your business. Even if your work doesn't involve client visits, the cleanliness of your environment affects the quality of what you produce. If you're unable to keep a baseline of clean in the space in which you operate, it becomes difficult to focus on your tasks. Eliminating the white noise from an untidy space will free up brain power to create quality work.

If you've read the last few paragraphs and failed to see where your home fits in, I invite you to consider the possibilities of a professional home. Your home may currently lack a professional purpose, but you will almost certainly define one at some point. For instance, if you are a member of a social club that rotates meeting locations and ends up at your home, you have created a professional purpose. When you volunteer for a community event, your home becomes the setting for other volunteers to gather and prep. If you're trying to recruit help for your service organization, your home turns into the informal meeting place where you win over new members.

When I sat down to make my own list of reasons why keeping a clean home is important to me, I found a mix of both personal and professional ones. I live in very close proximity to cousins, aunts, uncles, friends, and friendly neighbors. I also have a vacation rental out of a section of my home. When it came to managing the rental, I took the desires we all share when traveling and went from there. As I mentioned above, we all expect a clean environment when booking a hotel and rely on reviews to steer clear of unsavory accommodations. The same goes for private vacation rentals. Without the name brand to build trust and confidence, it's imperative to do everything possible to ensure a good review and high marks for cleanliness. After my first few bookings and high ratings, I found more requests hitting my inbox. The momentum kept up and so did my dedication to a clean space. I found that it didn't necessarily matter what color a bedspread was or if it matched the curtains. If people felt comfortable and clean in the space, they would say so and that would encourage potential customers to book.

Whether you use your property for personal or professional reasons, you'll find your "why" for keeping it clean. This book is here to help you put that "why" into action and start you on a journey to enjoying a clean home for years to come. Now that you're secure in your reasons and confident in your decision to make a change, let's tackle one of the biggest roadblocks to your clean future: anxiety.

If you're like me, you didn't receive a special education in cleaning and home maintenance. My grandmother, however, became my cleaning role model growing up. She was was classically trained to handle every aspect of house cleaning in addition to raising four children and working a full-time job.

As a kid, when gatherings and holidays were coming up, my parents and siblings would strive to get our house "Grandma Dot Clean." Even if I wasn't old enough to understand all my grandmother's tricks to a clean home, I knew the feeling of comfort and peace when walking through the door to a home like hers. It was a feeling that stuck.

Fast forward to college and summers working in the nation's capital. I was granted the immense privilege of staying in a family member's pied-a-terre during my summer internship. This responsibility became heavy, however, when I discovered my family would drop in without notice. After all, it was their place. But it switched something in me. I no longer had the cover of my upbringing or the excuse of a small dorm room to be messy. At that point, I only had the experience of cleaning houses for other people. I never established a routine for myself and my lifestyle. About to enter a new level of anxiety, I started small. I resolved to picking up after myself directly after using a space. After lounging on the couch watching TV, I'd make sure I folded the blanket and taken my water cup into the kitchen afterward. After making breakfast before work, I wiped every surface and cleaned each dish before I caught the bus.

That was how I made a turn away from cleaning anxiety and moved toward a zen-like attitude. We all have our own moments of anxiety around cleaning. You may have grown up in the cleanest house on the block, but found living on your own opened a sort of pandora's box of messiness. Whatever the case, it's important to start small. Picking up this book is the first small step. The next is a simple mind exercise.

To begin, find a comfy place to sit or lay down. You'll want to be able to relax each and every muscle. Next, take 10 slow breaths in and out. Breathe slowly and count each one to connect yourself with the rhythm. After your 10th breath, gather together the negative thoughts and associations with cleaning. Think of the failed attempts at establishing a routine. The seemingly endless task of keeping your home tidy. The embarrassment at paying guests or family members spotting dirt in your home. Think of the times you deep cleaned floors only to have a pet, child or partner create a mess soon after. Take all of those thoughts, memories, associations and acknowledge the negative feelings they inspire. Acknowledge those feelings and mentally send them on their way. Tell them they are no longer part of your present and have no place in your future.

Now, take 10 slow breaths in and out. Restore your body back to the relaxed state. After the 10th breath, imagine your home in its ideal state of cleanliness. The beds are made. The kitchen sink is empty. You can sit on your couch and see spotless floors into the next room. Immerse yourself in this vision by taking a mental tour of each room in your home, starting with the room you're in. Imagine what each room looks like perfectly clean. See the bedroom, bathroom, kitchen, living room, and even the closets. Don't miss out on the garage or storage closet, either. Take your time with this tour, absorb the positive feelings that swell within. Acknowledge those positive feelings that blossom during your mental tour. Invite them to stay and become part of your present and future.

Completing this mental exercise is just the beginning of the positive effects cleaning can have on your overall health. The simple act of envisioning a clean home helps put you in a mental state where you not only can function, but flourish in your cleaning routine. I mentioned a UCLA study in the introduction that found a relationship between clean homes and what owners say about their homes. The cleaner and more organized a home, the more positive things a homeowner had to say. The findings seem rational and matter-of-fact, but the simplicity of that connection is often overshadowed by the many ways cleaning can feel like an unwanted chore.

One way in which cleaning itself can help us step away from anxiety is through using cleaning as a mental break from our other work. In fact, a study from Florida State University found that mindfully washing dishes can calm the brain and decrease the stress you feel. The key word is "mindfully." Just as you tackled worrying thoughts and anxiety around cleaning, you can take on the act of cleaning itself with a bit of relaxed awareness.

The study focused on dishwashing, which for some people remains the most trying of household chores. However, the tactics of mindfulness can easily be applied to everything on your checklist. Carefully making your bed in the morning can help awaken your brain. It also gives you the first accomplishment for the day. With that achievement reached, you approach your work and other tasks with confidence. Rhythmically sweeping the floors or gliding the vacuum across them offers a repetitive physical motion that allows your brain to work on a mental problem. Whether stoking a creative flame or seeking an answer to a logic problem at work, the action gets blood flowing. At the end of the task, you may still be seeking the answer but will have found immediate accomplishment in the clean floors beneath your feet.

By now, you may either be feeling relaxed for the next steps or questioning how mental exercises translate into a clean home. Perhaps you're feeling a mix of both. The simple answer to both of those reactions is: I'll show you how. This book and every strategy within is more than just a random collection of factoids, anecdotes, and studies. It's the total guide to home cleaning that you'll refer to again and again. It's the encouraging friend who walks with you on a fulfilling journey. It's exactly what you need to start small and arrive at your final, clean destination.

Chapter 2: The Best Supplies For Every Surface

I have lived in 10 different rooms or apartments from the beginning of college to my home now. Each home or apartment was a different age with varying finishes and fixtures. Some were well cared for and required general cleaning. Others required deep cleaning and a trip to the hardware store to make them habitable. Each situation required its own set of cleaning supplies that worked best for the surfaces within. I developed this chapter using what I learned from my experience. There's a recommendation of products throughout starting with the most versatile, all-purpose cleaners. In the following chapter, I'll share my best recipes for homemade products. You should choose what works best for you and your home. This chapter is here to provide you with options.

All-Purpose Cleaners

These are first in the chapter because of their versatility. They can work in any room on most surfaces.

Method All-Purpose Cleaner® in various scents:

The choice in scents is plentiful and allows you to match the aroma to your preferences. According to the manufacturer, it is suited for most non-porous surfaces. When applied to a greasy kitchen countertop or toothpaste-laden bathroom sink, it performed admirably. This cleaner is not suited for grime build-up without the use of tools. It is possible to use too much at once, making the surface feel grimy from the cleaner and in need of a wipe down with a dry cloth. A key benefit is that it's non-toxic, which is naturally derived from biodegradable ingredients. With this benefit, it's an excellent choice for RV's, camping and homes with children and pets.

Trader Joe's Cedarwood and Sage All-Purpose Cleaner®:

Trader Joe's delivers on an affordable cleaning product without the unnatural looking neon color found in similarly priced cleaners. The scent is pleasant, but not overpowering. It does especially well on mirrors and windows. It performs its purpose without you worrying about putting too much on and leaving a new layer of cleaner grime. It's handy on non-porous surfaces such as sealed dining room tables, easily lifting dinner leftovers. It is also a plant based cleaner and biodegradable.

Mrs. Meyer's Multi-Surface Everyday Cleaner®:

The entire line of Mrs. Meyer's cleaners provides aromatherapy in addition to cleaning. The all-purpose cleaner comes in a variety of scents and the product performs well in most every application. Even if it can't remove all soap scum, it does leave it cleaner than before. One of the best parts of this cleaner is that you can purchase refills that are concentrated. This means less weight from excess water during shipping. The green trend continues with this product as it uses all biodegradable ingredients and sustainable sources wherever possible.

Purell Multi-Surface® Cleaner:

The name most associated with hand sanitizer applied the logic of sterilizing hands to the surfaces in your home. It is alcohol-based, requiring that it be used on non-porous surfaces. However, it doesn't need to be wiped down after use like other cleaners including Lysol® disinfecting wipes. It kills germs on contact, without needing you to wipe them away. This product is amazing in bathrooms, mud rooms, garages, and kitchens. Just be mindful of the surfaces!

Bathroom

Let's begin with the room that can be sanitized to hospital standards right after scrubbing but becomes a health hazard if not regularly cleaned. It's important to your family's health to keep a clean bathroom and even more important for vacation rental guests. Even if bathrooms are "clean," lurking rust stains, mildew spots, or soap buildup is a bad look for you and for your guests. The products used to clean should not only tackle grime and soap scum, but disinfect most if not all surfaces. There are a few tools you'll need to get the job done efficiently and quickly.

Solid Surfaces:

These surfaces are usually made of composite materials like Corian® or plastic veneer.
- Avoid abrasive materials if your surface was finished in a semi-gloss or gloss
- A non-greasy all-purpose cleaner will keep these surfaces clean
- If residue builds up, wipe down with a bleach cleaner like Soft Scrub®

MUST HAVE TOOL: Keep multiple rags in the same color closeby to wipe down surfaces after use. This will stave off deep cleans saving you time and effort down the road.

Acrylic:

Used for sinks, vanity tops, and showers, this surface is easy to clean and retains its new-in-box look for much longer than other materials like tile.
- This is one surface that needs disinfection
- After cleaning with a non-greasy all-purpose cleaner, wipe down with vinegar or bleach for disinfection
- Use a toothbrush to clean edges and caulk lines

MUST HAVE TOOL: Mr. Clean® Magic Eraser removes discolorations from soap scum with ease. Look for store brand equivalents to save a few dollars.

Stone and Granite:

Marble, quartz, granite, and limestone are the most common stone surface materials.
- Invest in a cleaner specific for stone and granite
- Always wipe down the surface after using a cleaner
- Marble and Granite: Take It For Granite® cleaner covers everything from floors to countertops
- Quartz: Use a window cleaner or all-purpose cleaner
- Limestone: Caldrea® Countertop Spray is perfect for non-porous surfaces like natural stone
- Use microfiber cloths to avoid scratches on all these surfaces

MUST HAVE TOOL: Razor blades make it easy to remove mineral stains and stuck on mess. Gently pass over the stains or mess several times until it wears down. Clean as usual.

Porcelain, Other Ceramics, and Cast Iron:

Old homes have cast iron sinks and tubs that may or may not need resealing. You can get either clean with the products below.
- Porcelain: an abrasive cleaner like Mrs. Meyers® Surface Scrub works wonders on set-in stains
- Toilets and bidets: a disinfecting cleaner like Method® Antibac Toilet gets rid of germs without the chemical smell using citric acid
- Tubs: A bleach cleaner like Soft Scrub® accomplishes a deep clean while an all-purpose cleaner is suitable for a regular cleaning

- Unsealed tubs and sinks: These get dirty, fast. Soft Scrub® or a vinegar baking soda mixture will take out stains until you can reseal

MUST HAVE TOOL: Use the following brushes for the best cleaning.
1. A toothbrush or similarly sized brush for small spaces
2. A handled stiff brush to cover more surface area.
3. A long-handled stiff brush to use leverage against a tough stain

EXTRA MUST HAVE TOOL: Keep a squeegee in your shower! This handy tool will keep soap from building up on tile, acrylic, and any other bath wall surface.

Faucets:

Nickel, chrome, brass, bronze, and stainless steel are the most common faucet finishes. They often come in either brushed or satin (shiny) variations. They can all use a wipe down with a cleaning rag after use to help prevent buildup and keep them sparkling between cleans. For grime and dirt removal, find an all-purpose cleaner that can disinfect without leaving residue behind. Try Purell Multi-Surface® Cleaner.

One common nuisance is the buildup of minerals where the faucet meets the sink or shower. It starts small and grows creeping out onto the surface of the sink or shower. Use an old toothbrush to scrub it during your regular cleaning. To get yourself to a baseline state of no buildup, use a metal cuticle tool found in nail grooming kits to gently scrape the buildup away.

Kitchen:

Depending on your lifestyle, the kitchen may be the most used room in your home. If you have one in your vacation rental, guests will use it for breakfasts and the occasional quick meal. It's perfectly normal for a kitchen to look lived in. Hardly anyone will strive to put away the dish drying rack between uses, but everyone can keep it empty after use.

Kitchen Surfaces

Stainless Steel:

Used for appliance faces, sinks and even countertops.
- The surface can be scratched, avoid abrasive tools and cleaners
- To get a streak-free clean on appliances and counters, use a stainless steel specific cleaner and don't be afraid to buff the surface with a soft cloth after cleaning
- Stainless sinks are susceptible to water marks if food, dishes, and water is left too long
- Make sure you wash dishes and rinse your sink soon after use to prevent marks

Porcelain-enameled:

Often found in the form of the popular farmhouse style sink.
- Avoid steel wool or scouring pads to protect the finish
- A plastic bristle brush is perfect for stains or stuck-on food
- For a deep-clean, use a gel cleaner that can sit and tackle stains like Mrs Meyers® Gel Cleaner or Soft Scrub®

Solid Surface:

Brand-name countertops, finishes on appliances, sinks, and vinyl laminate flooring.
- Avoid abrasive materials if your surface was finished in a semi-gloss or gloss
- A non-greasy all-purpose cleaner will keep these surfaces clean
- If residue builds up, wipe down with a bleach cleaner like Soft Scrub®

Tile:
May be used in countertops, backsplash, and flooring.
- Wipe down tile countertops after use to prevent grout stains
- A cleaner like Black Diamond® Marble and Tile will remove dirt and stains without leaving residue
- Backsplashes see a lot of food particles and should be wiped down after preparing and cooking food to prevent set-in stains

Stone and Granite:
Marble, quartz, granite, and limestone are the most common.
- Invest in a cleaner made for a stone surface
- Always wipe down the surface after using a cleaner
- Marble and Granite: Take It For Granite® cleaner covers everything from floors to countertops
- Quartz: Use a window cleaner or all-purpose cleaner
- Limestone: Caldrea® Countertop Spray is perfect for non-porous surfaces like natural stone
- Use microfiber cloths to provide extra softness to these surfaces

Wood:
Butcher blocks, counter tops, and even floors.
- Whether stand-alone or built into your countertop, butcher blocks need special care
- Howard® Butcher Block conditioner is food grade and should be applied regularly based on your use to keep the wood safe from food and other stains
- Wood floors in kitchens will already be sealed, but can be protected from accidental drops of heavy items (like mixing bowls or plates) with coordinating accent rugs

Favorite Kitchen Tools

Bona® mop kits:

Bona® makes simple non-smelly cleaners for your wood and tile surfaces making it the easiest system to use on all solid surface floors in your home. You can purchase multiple mopping pads to be able to clean all your floors in one go without leaving dirt behind. Throw them in the washer on a hot water cycle with regular laundry detergent. They're much more convenient than disposable ones and create less waste. You can also find generic versions of the mop, pads, and cleaner on janitor supply store websites. I recommend having a mop set (mop, a few pads, spray bottle of cleaner) on each level of your home or in each solid surface room.

Razor Blades:

Razor blades work exceptionally well on stuck burnt food on glass top ranges and even granite countertops. Be sure to go slowly and gently on surfaces that can scratch. Run the blade with light pressure back and forth over the stuck-on mess until it's broken up enough to remove with a soft cloth.

Cleaning Rags:

These will save your wallet on buying paper towels and plenty of trees. Make a set of at least 30 for your kitchen using old towels or t-shirts. If you can, choose one color to use in the kitchen and another color for any other room they're used in. This makes it easier to sort at laundry time and keep your bathroom rags from ending up in your kitchen.

Sink Grates:

Made of metal or silicone, sink grates sit at the bottom of your sink and keep dishes from directly touching the surface. This will not only keep your sink cleaner for longer, but protect any sealing on a new sink from wearing down sooner than it should.

Under Sink Storage:

Many kitchens now have intricate storage drawers, baskets, and more inside each cabinet. Even if you don't have sophisticated organization in other parts of your kitchen, invest in under sink storage. Specifically, a wire drawer made in a U-shape to avoid any plumbing and can slide out for a clear view of your supplies. This is a game changer for any kitchen. It's one of the most used rooms in the house, and thus, the most cleaned. You owe it to yourself to make finding supplies and tools easier.

Appliances

There were some appliances that fell under the surface categories above, but I want to dedicate a small section to everything that didn't fit there.

Ovens and Ranges:

If you have a gas range and find the cast iron grates difficult to clean, try a soak in hot water and dish detergent (like Dawn®) for 15 minutes before applying something like Goo Gone® Grill and Grate cleaner with a nylon or other plastic scouring pad. Ceramic grates can be soaked in the same solution and then scrubbed with a plastic-bristle brush to break up stains.

Refrigerators:

As soon as I learned you could take all the shelves and drawers out of a fridge, mine has never looked better – and for longer! Cleaning is simple with a plastic bristle brush and dish detergent. While the shelves are out, I warm up some wet rags in my microwave, put on some gloves and let the heat go to work cleaning off the worst food stains. After that, I take a disinfecting cleaner like Soft Scrub® or Purell® to wipe down the inside of the fridge. If you avoid cleaning your freezer because you think you have to let it thaw out completely, take advantage of the microwave and warm up wet rags. If ice buildup is especially thick, bring water to almost a boil on the stove and slowly pour into the bottom of the freezer where the build up occurred. This melts everything so you can quickly mop it up with a large towel.

Small Appliances:

My best trick to keeping these clean is storing them off the counter. I found myself constantly wiping down the mixer after preparing dinner, and I hadn't even used it in my prep! If that's not possible, designate a section of countertop that is only for food prep. Chopping, mixing and combining can all be done in one place while appliances live on other parts of the counter. Investing in a sturdy food cover will prevent spills while cooking.

Living Spaces:

Living rooms, home offices, and playrooms are some of the most common living spaces. They provide specific uses to make our time at home more enjoyable and productive.

Carpets and Rugs:

Carpet is a cozy choice for living spaces and easy to take care of with the right tools and tricks. For daily cleaning, invest in a good vacuum. It doesn't need to be a Dyson® either. I have found great success on low-pile and high-pile carpets with my Shark Navigator® Lift-Away® upright vacuum cleaner. It is economical and bagless (one less thing to keep on your shopping list). The canister design also makes it easy to clean with soap and water. It comes with a HEPA filter, in addition to, a sponge filter you can wash out every three months. A vacuum is only as good as the maintenance done to it, so no matter the brand follow the user's manual to ensure that each part is getting the recommended maintenance at the appropriate intervals. Invest in the accessories, too. You'll want a dust wand, an upholstery tool, and hose extensions for high ceilings.

What about hardwood or vinyl floors? I recommend a small canister vacuum like Eureka® Mighty Mite. It is a bag vacuum, but also one of the most effective vacuums in terms of suction and durability. I have had my vacuum for almost 10 years now and it still picks up pet hair, dust, and crumbs like a champ.

Rugs:

Rugs come in all price ranges thanks to improved manufacturing techniques and more affordable materials. Most store bought rugs will do fine with regular vacuuming and spot cleaning using Woolite® carpet cleaner. You can also take your rugs to be professionally cleaned every few years. For deep cleaning on wool rugs, professional cleaning is the only option because traditional methods (rented steam cleaners) leave too much water and can damage the wool. If you do have a stain on a wool rug, blot it (don't rub) with tepid water and a clean white towel.

Upholstered Furniture:

The fabric used on furniture is typically much more durable than the fabric used to make our clothing. It is also an item where you gain more durability and a longer lifespan as the price increases. Whether you have

IKEA® furniture or the latest from West Elm®, it's easy to keep them clean.

Most upholstery fabric will be blends of cotton, wool, and synthetic fibers. For those with leather, Mohawk® has a complete leather care and cleaning kit to tackle light surface scratches and discoloration.

For all other upholstery fabric, Woolite® makes a great upholstery cleaner to handle stains. To keep the fabric fresh and clear out any scents it absorbed, a spray of vinegar on the fabric will take on odors. Test a small area before spraying the rest of the upholstery. If you can remove cushion covers or any other fabric, wash on a delicate cycle using either Woolite® regular detergent or Woolite® Darks. These detergents will help keep the color in place so cushions that have been washed don't look a shade different from the rest of the upholstery.

Wooden or Veneer Furniture:

The product needed to care for wood furniture (and make it last for centuries) is so simple that most everyone overlooks it. All you need is a damp soft cloth that can be from an old towel or t-shirt. Wipe down each side of the wood and make sure to get in to each crevice to remove dust buildup. There are many wood cleaners marketed as must-haves but the reality is, wood is an easy clean. It doesn't need all of the fancy ingredients to make it shine. In fact, using cleaners like Pledge® and others actually builds up residue over time making your furniture look dull. Once a year (and only once a year), I will apply Old English® as a sort of extra barrier to dust and dirt. Other than that, it's a damp soft cloth for routine cleaning.

If your kitchen table is wood and you need to disinfect, use a solution of water and vinegar to spray it down. The ratio should be ¼ cup of vinegar to ¾ cup water. For painted wood, use a gentle all-purpose cleaner to remove spots and grime before wiping down with a damp soft cloth and letting it dry.

Lighting:

For fabric shades, use a dust wand vacuum attachment to take up the pet hair or dust that's collected. A lint roller (or traditional lint brush) can work well depending on the shape of the lamp shade.

For metal or glass sconces, remove them (if possible) and wipe them down with an all-purpose cleaner that doesn't leave streaks. If you can't remove them, grab your step stool and rise to them for cleaning.

Accessories:

I have to talk a little bit about plants because they are their own kind of cleaner. They keep indoor air from becoming polluted and bring in color to any room. Basic maintenance of plants is what I recommend to keep the area of the room they're in clean. Remove dead or dying leaves, branches and stems when they appear. This will prevent you having to vacuum them up later. Make sure the plants have a drainage plate or similar, if the species requires it. Keep them out of reach of pets to avoid them snacking on leaves and leaving a mess behind.

Anything not put away in a cabinet (printers, toys, figurines, vases, etc) requires some attention on a regular basis in order to avoid more intensive cleaning down the road. Invest in a microfiber duster and a few extra pads so you can dust these items at least once a week. Keeping the dust off of them now prevents it from building up and mixing with the moisture in the air to create a sort of dust icing. When it builds up to the dust icing point, you'll need a moist cloth and some time to wipe down each item.

Bedroom

Bed:

Your bed will most likely take up the biggest surface area, which means there's a lot of floor underneath that doesn't get attention when you vacuum. If you have the additional hose extensions for your vacuum, you should be able to reach underneath your bed. If your bed is particularly low or hard to reach, you may want to consider an area rug to put underneath. This will allow dirt, hair, and dust to get caught on the outer edges of the carpet before they reach under the bed.

Bedside Tables:

I advocate for bedside tables with drawers to keep necessary items close at hand and out of sight for a cleaner look. However, glasses, phones, and jewelry can somehow end up scattered on top. If that's the case with you, keep all other clutter off these surfaces and make space for these items. A small decorative jewelry tray keeps rings and other loose items safe. I also recommend a Diamond Dazzle® stick to dust off jewelry.

Room for your phone becomes designated with a wireless charging pad. The case you brought your glasses home with becomes a safe place for spectacles. In order to keep these items clean and organized, stock cleaning pads for your phone and microfiber cloth for glasses. Cleaning these often-used items daily will keep germs away and your vision clear.

Curtains, Blinds, and Shutters:

You more than likely have window coverings in every room of your house, but they're especially necessary in bedrooms. Keep them in top shape, whether in the bedroom or living room.

Fabric Curtains:

For any visible dust, use the dust wand attachment on your vacuum while holding the curtain to gently vacuum up dust. Once a year, you can air out the curtains in the sun or put them in the dryer for a 20 minute cycle. If they are washable, feel free to also wash them before airing out.

Blinds and Shutters:

For deep cleaning, I recommend a warm bowl of water and vinegar applied gently with soft cloths. It is tedious, but if you keep up with regular dusting, you'll be able to go longer between these deep cleans. Using a microfiber duster, you can safely swipe between each blind without damage. You'll be able to pick up a lot with the microfiber as you perform this task.

Bedding:

As dirt collects on us and our pets, it's important to wash your sheets once a week. Dirt and dust buildup on sheets can irritate skin and aggravate allergies. Duvet covers should also be washed weekly while duvet inserts can be washed once a year. If possible, change your shower routine to the evenings to keep your sheets fresh all week long.

Air:

If you're getting the recommended 8 hours of sleep, that's ⅓ of your day spent in your bedroom. Clean air is especially important in this room where so much time is spent. Add houseplants to help clean the air and invest in a quiet air purifier to really keep the air fresh

Small Spaces:

Entryways, hallways, mudrooms, and other small spaces also need attention. Wherever possible, I like to use cleaners and tools across multiple rooms. In that spirit, you'll find the recommendations for surfaces you have in these spaces by referring back to other rooms in the chapter. However, there are some unique tips and tools for small spaces.

Machine washable rugs in high-traffic areas like entryways, hallways, and mudrooms are a must to keep stains away (and your mind at ease). Machine washable rugs also tend to be a bit more affordable than other kinds, allowing you to pick up a few extra rugs to rotate and keep your floors covered at all times. For every rug in a high-traffic area, I recommend having one backup.

Upright canister vacuums work wonders in these spaces. Because of their high-traffic nature, dirt from the outside builds up quicker than elsewhere in the house. By keeping one of these vacuums in the nearest coat closet, you can quickly clean up any dirt.

There are new cleaning products hitting shelves and social media advertisements everyday. When researching and trying out new products, I often wished there was someone who could just tell me what to use in each scenario. This chapter is my own version of that much sought-after advice and the rest of the book builds on it. By the time you finish this book, you'll no longer wonder what to use and where.

If you went out and bought everything in this chapter today you'd likely blow your cleaning budget for the entire year. To avoid that, take in these new products slowly. You may already have a great vacuum, but maybe it needs some TLC. Skip the new vacuum and go right for the set of cleaners that will make your bathroom sparkle. For any old products, make sure you dispose of them properly in a local hazardous waste recycling center.

Chapter 3: DIY Cleaning Mixes

Your cleaning supplies storage may look like a disaster right now. It may be one of the biggest reasons you committed to changing how you clean. It's so easy to pick up a spray bottle from the alluring display at the end of the store aisle. You might have tried a product based on a recommendation from a friend but found it useless. These products stack up under sinks and in closets. I committed to using up all the products I had in my home. When that wasn't possible, I properly disposed of any leftover items (following my local hazardous waste disposal guidelines).

I urge you to do the same and work your way through the stacks of ineffective cleaners, replacing each one with recipes found in this chapter and the store-bought items from the previous chapter. Taken together, the list of products provides choice for every household cleaning need. There are mothers who worry about using bleach in the same bathtub they bathe their children. There are new apartment dwellers who are stuck with the unfortunate task of deep cleaning a bathroom that was previously neglected. Each phase of our life will require different products. The cleaning recipes in this chapter fit a multitude of applications. They also are easy on your budget and use ingredients you can find in grocery stores.

Cleaning Ingredients:

The recipes in this chapter all take ingredients from this list. Feel free to use it as a shopping list and stock up.

- Lemon juice
- Distilled white vinegar
- Baking soda
- Borax
- Bleach
- Isopropyl alcohol
- Natural dish soap
- Glycerin
- Olive oil

Cleaning Recipes

Bathroom

Bathrooms are one of the most important rooms to sanitize. The recipes I've found keep that in mind and offer non-chemical options to disinfect surfaces. I've also included a few that will get you to a basic level of clean you can easily maintain.

The-Stains-Are-Not-Mine Grout Cleaning Recipe:
- 1tbsp of baking soda
- ½ tbsp bleach

This recipe is great for tile in bathrooms and kitchens. Because it uses bleach, I mix the ingredients together in the amounts listed creating a small amount of paste. Drip that or scoop with your scrub brush onto the grout. Most stains will scrub out immediately, but if needed, let the mix sit for 10 minutes before trying to scrub. I highly recommend this method when moving into a new home or apartment. You can also do it as preparation for re-sealing your grout, which should be done periodically to prevent deep set stains and prolong the life of the grout.

Everyday Cleaning Tile and Grout Recipe:
- 2 cups water
- 2 cups vinegar
- 1tbsp natural dish soap

Mix the water and vinegar together in a spray bottle before adding the dish soap.

This recipe is perfect for weekly tile and grout cleaning in your bathroom. It also works well cleaning the backsplash in your kitchen. It will remove soap scum in your bathroom while tackling food grease buildup in your kitchen.

Tip: If you have unglazed tiles that are more textured, you'll need a recipe that can tackle the dirt inside all the nooks and crannies. Mix half a cup of baking soda into a bucket of warm water (about a gallon) and wipe down with a soft cloth letting the baking soda do the scrubbing.

Water Scale Rescue:
- ¼ cup vinegar
- ¾ cup hot water (not boiling)
- 1 tbsp natural dish soap

Mix all ingredients together in spray bottle. Spray the fixture or area and let soak for 5 minutes before rinsing. Wash shower liners with vinegar and hot water in your washing machine to get the same effect

Hard-To-Reach Cleaner:

- 1 cup lemon juice

Dip a toothbrush into lemon juice to clean grime and water marks inside the metal tracks of shower doors, on shower curtain rods, and other shower door hardware.

Mineral Deposit Remover:

- Varying amounts of vinegar

Whether on your faucets or showerhead, a soak in straight vinegar will loosen deposits and allow you to scrub them away with a toothbrush or straight pin.

Toilet Cleaner:

- 1/2 cup of white vinegar

Utilize the disinfectant properties of white vinegar for everyday toilet cleaning. If cleaning up a ring where the water meets the bowl, let a half cup of vinegar sit for a few hours before scrubbing.

Kitchen

Preparing raw meat and produce both require a sanitized environment to protect your health. These recipes keep that in mind with simple ingredients and easy applications. I also included a few recipes that took me years to find, including one to clean your oven. My favorite is the all-purpose disinfecting cleaner that can be made with any desired scent using essential oils.

All-Purpose Disinfecting Cleaner:

- ½ cup water
- ½ cup white vinegar
- 2 tbsp fresh lemon juice (you can substitute 12-24 drops of a preferred essential oil for the lemon juice)

This cleaner is perfect for the kitchen (and bathroom) because it not only cuts grease, but can disinfect. This is essential in any kitchen that is prepping raw food.

Note: Vinegar will dull the shine of granite and other stone countertops. Mix a recipe of half water and half isopropyl alcohol to disinfect and clean granite while protecting the surface.

Ultimate Non-Abrasive Disinfecting Oven Cleaner:

- 2 cups baking soda
- ½ cup borax

Store dry mix in a glass container. Sprinkle onto oven mess and then spray area with water from a spray bottle. Scrub with a plastic bristle brush.

Marble Counter Cleaner:

- ⅓ cup liquid fabric softener
- ⅔ cup water.

Mix ingredients together in a spray bottle and apply to marble surface, wipe clean with a cloth, and then polish with a soft cloth.

Living Areas

Living areas include everything from dining rooms to bedrooms and even the laundry room. These recipes help to tackle dirt on windows, floors, and even inside washing machines.

Spot-Free Window Cleaner:

- 2 cups water
- ¼ cup vinegar.

Mix ingredients in a spray bottle. Spray windows and wipe down with a reusable cloth.

Tip: If you've been cleaning your windows with store-bought cleaners, they more than likely contain ingredients that build up into a wax film on your windows. It may take several cleanings, and cloths to get this layer of wax off and your windows sparkling.

Non-Wood Floor Cleaner:

- ¼ cup natural liquid soap
- ½ cup vinegar
- 2 gallons of hot water

Combine all ingredients. If using a traditional mop, mix ingredients in a bucket. If using a dry mop, combine into spray bottles. This recipe is perfect for vinyl, linoleum, and even tile.

Wood Floor Cleaner:

- ¼ cup natural liquid soap
- ½ cup glycerin
- 2 gallons of hot water.

Combine all ingredients. If using a traditional mop, mix ingredients in a bucket. If using a dry mop, combine into spray bottles.

Tip: Try a natural liquid soap with essential oils in it for an even better smell and some aromatherapy while cleaning.

Deep Carpet Cleaner:

- ⅛ cup natural liquid soap
- 2 gallons of water
- Add ½ tsp of borax to tackle especially dirty carpets.

This formula is meant for use in professional or home carpet cleaners. It gives you an effective cleaner with less chemicals than standard concentrates. You can also add essential oils for a fresh scent.

Tip: Rent a carpet cleaner from a local retailer and use this formula to save $15-20 on the retailer's cleaning concentrate.

Wood Furniture Polish:

- 2 cups olive oil
- 1 cup lemon juice.

Mix ingredients in a bowl. Apply with a soft cloth to lessen scratches before buffing with a different soft cloth.

Washing Machine Sanitizer:

- 1 and 1/4 cup vinegar
- 1 quick clean cycle with hot water.

Pour 1 cup vinegar directly into washer drum and ¼ cup vinegar into soap dispenser. Wash on a quick wash cycle (about 30 minutes) with hot water.

After reading this chapter, you'll be amazed at what can be tackled with less than 10 ingredients. I hand selected each recipe based on its own impact in my home and because I believe in owning cleaners with less chemicals. In some cases, heavy-duty cleaners like bleach are needed to get a room back to a clean state. In those cases, make sure the area is well-ventilated and look into a mask that will help filter any fumes or smells from the cleaner. Once an area is back to basic cleanliness, use these recipes to keep them sparkling.

Chapter 4: Decluttering Steps You Can't Skip

Gathering the right cleaners, recipes, and tools is the beginning of a great cleaning experience. The next step is to declutter each area in preparation for cleaning. Even the most dedicated person will have some clutter to move around in each room before beginning their cleaning regimen. To avoid getting caught up in the mess and losing precious time picking things up, make decluttering part of your routine. Give yourself a set amount of time when cleaning each room to take care of things left behind from previous use. Each room has a list of tips to follow and when completed together, take less than 10 minutes. It's the perfect warmup before cleaning begins.

Bathroom

Designate a Cleaning Basket: Your bathroom may have multiple drawers and cabinets making it easy to store frequently used items out of sight. You may also keep a certain number of products and tools on your counter or sink for easy access. No matter the setup, the quickest way to declutter a bathroom is by using a plastic basket. Placing all the products and tools into the basket keeps them in one place while cleaning. When finished, you can take each item out individually, giving you a moment to notice if a bottle is empty or if an item belongs in another room. This same method also applies for cleaning your bath or shower.

Keep a Hamper in Sight: A hamper in the bathroom may already be part of your home organization. If not, make it happen. Quickly decluttering clothes in your bathroom depends on ease of storage. A nearby hamper organizes your clothes ready to be washed and allows you to start cleaning faster.

Make Room for Jewelry and Watches: It's easy to have jewelry and watches pile up in a bathroom. They begin to stack up on countertops, the backs of toilets, and on shelves. Designate one spot to keep jewelry worn frequently, preferably in a jewelry box.

Take Out the Trash: Remove the liner from your bathroom trashcan and pick up loose trash on counters, floors, and shelves. After taking out the trash, you avoid having to stop the cleaning process to pick up peeled product labels, beauty store receipts, and product packaging.

Kitchen

It's easy for a kitchen to look like it's been neglected for a week after just one meal. If you gave yourself the night off and wake up in the morning needing to get it back in shape, don't worry. Follow these steps and you'll have a clean kitchen in no time.

Stack the Dishes: The only time my sink, dishwasher, and dish rack are empty of dishes is for an hour after the Thanksgiving meal. With so many cooks in the kitchen preparing a feast fit for the holiday, you get an equal amount of cleaners. Every dish is washed, dried, and put away before the holiday football game reaches halftime. But this only happens once a year. On days that are not Thanksgiving, it's important to not be overwhelmed by dishes standing between you and cleaning your kitchen. If your sink is nearly empty, grab all the dirty dishes around the kitchen and stack them in the sink. If your sink is full, empty the dishwasher or dish rack and set a time for 5 minutes to wash (or load as many dishes as you can). This clears your counters and lets you tackle the full task of emptying the sink at the end of your cleaning regimen. With the rest of the kitchen clean, you can't help but tackle the dishes and finish off the space.

Move from Left to Right: Most kitchen counters have temporary clutter like cereal boxes or other food. They also have more permanent clutter including utensil holders and small appliances. To truly tackle every spot of counter space, start on the farthest left section of counter. Move all clutter to a section of counter on the right. Clean the bare counter and then replace the appliances and other items. Start on the far left and use the left to right motion to give you momentum until the space is clean. Avoid moving countertop clutter to a kitchen table or to a designated spot on the other side of the kitchen, as it is more time consuming.

Get Rid of Papers: Printed recipes, mail, and magazines can stack up quickly in a kitchen. Before you can start cleaning, you need to gather all the paper in the kitchen in one spot to sort later. Find a basket or small bin and go around the space to find all the paper. If you find items that belong in different rooms, put them together in their own separate basket to be sorted later. These baskets are not a new version of a junk drawer. Instead, they offer a quick way to corral items before sorting them.

Pick Up Pet Bowls: Food and water bowls for pets are often found in the kitchen. Before you begin cleaning, take up the bowls and put them in the sink. If you're taking time to clean the kitchen, it's also a great opportunity to clean out the food and water bowls for your pets.

Living Room

Your living room can end up being the catchall for everything that doesn't belong. This includes coats that should be on the coat rack or in the mud room. A pile of clean laundry that got stuck on the way from the dryer to your dresser drawers. Empty boxes from mail delivery. Books, bags, and even shoes that ended up tucked into corners. This may be the most daunting room to clean because of the immense buildup of clutter. Strip that title away with these simple tips (and a mindful touch).

Bring-Your-Own Trash Can: Save yourself time and trouble by bringing in a lined wastebasket before you even begin cleaning. It is crucial to keep with you while carrying out the following tips.

Mail, Magazines, Memorabilia: Remember the basket you used for decluttering paper in the kitchen? It should be empty now and ready to collect postcards, open letters, and random paper building up in the living room. Go through the room picking up each piece of paper and immediately tossing useless ones in the wastebasket. If you're not sure if a paper or magazine is worth keeping, put it in the basket. The goal of this decluttering method is to do it quickly. Save the thoroughness for when you're emptying the basket of paper.

Choose a Back (Chair or Couch): You've already spent time bringing in a trash can and a basket to collect clutter. Don't waste anymore time by bringing in a clothes hamper, too. Take any coats, clothes, or blankets and lay them in a pile on a chair or section of the couch. Move them during cleaning when you need to reach the section they're on before sorting them at the end.

Toys and More Toys: Whether you have human children, animal children, or a combination of both, toys are a natural accessory to the space. In the living room, they can take up large sections of floor making it impossible to carry on with your cleaning. Each living room should have a toy basket to not only teach children the necessary task of tidying up, but to easily collect toys before cleaning.

<u>Bedroom</u>

The items you keep in your bedroom typically have a home. Jewelry boxes keep precious pieces safe. Dressers store non-hanging clothes. A vanity table collects the perfumes and beauty products used daily. It's more than easy, however, for these items to end up all over the room.

The best and most simple way to declutter a bedroom is by first ensuring each bedroom item has a home. Then, when preparing to clean, set a time for 10 minutes to put as many things back in their homes as possible. For items that don't belong in the bedroom, use the same decluttering basket from the kitchen and living room to store the items in one place. After cleaning, take them to their designated spots in the rest of your home.

Laundry Room

It's so easy to take even the most organized laundry room and turn it into a disaster over the course of normal use. Before getting down to cleaning spilled soap and runaway lint, take a moment to pick up clutter.

Clothes: Keep an extra hamper in your laundry room, preferably one that folds flat. Use it to gather together the random assortment of line dried clothes, loose socks, and other linen. Empty it after cleaning to get each item back to its home.

Cleaning Products: While you may not keep all the cleaning products for your home in the laundry room, the ones that do live there are probably in bins or loose on shelves. You may even store them in baskets that are then placed on those same shelves. No matter the case, when it's time to deep clean and wipe down their storage, get them on the floor. Starting with the highest shelf or basket, remove all products and place them on the floor. Moving from top to bottom keeps dust and dirt from falling off a higher shelf to a lower one you just cleaned.

Home Office

Your home office may be the epicenter of productivity and still look like the aftermath of an earthquake. It's important to keep this area clean, especially if you work from home. Keeping dirt and dust down in this room helps keep the air healthy while you're putting in hours for work.

The quickest way to declutter in preparation for cleaning is with designated baskets. One for papers, one for books and one for items that belong elsewhere. Use the baskets from the kitchen and living room to cut down on extra baskets laying around that force you to empty them after each use. Collect papers from all over the room in one basket. Take books that need reshelving or magazines that need categorizing and put them in another basket. If you have items that belong in a different room like an item of clothing, shoes, blanket or other, gather them in one basket. At the end of cleaning, take this basket around the house until each item has found its home again.

Decluttering a space before cleaning is most often an exercise in triage. You're doing what you can with the time you have to achieve the best possible result. When you start out on the journey to find a regular cleaning schedule for your home, it will feel overwhelming. That's okay. You are building a routine to last you a lifetime and that doesn't happen overnight. The decluttering tips in this chapter are meant to get you over one of the biggest hurdles on your way to a lifetime cleaning routine: the piles of clutter that exist now. Your cleaning routine may one day skip most if not all of these decluttering tips. You might find yourself doing dishes as you use them preventing a pile-up in the sink. You might begin sorting mail at the mailbox keeping junk out and important items filed away immediately. You will find the balance that works for you and your lifestyle. In the meantime, this chapter is everything you need to get started today. Remember that starting small means you're already on your way to big things.

Chapter 5: Kitchen

A kitchen often serves as the center of a home. Even small kitchens draw family and friends during meal preparation and clean up. Even when you're not entertaining, the space serves you and your family throughout the day. Despite the heavy use, it's one of the easiest rooms in your home to keep clean. Unlike other rooms in your home, the messes created in the kitchen are easily tackled while working on other important tasks. When cooking most everyday meals, there is inevitably downtime during the process. While waiting for water to boil for pasta, you can stir the pasta sauce before unloading or loading the dishwasher. When I've finally assembled vegetables for roasting, hit the button to start the timer and finish not only meal prep cleanup but the daily wipedown of all the counters.

Thanks to the ease of multitasking in the kitchen, this chapter is especially motivating and provides a number of ways to make best use of your time. In this chapter and the ones after, I've organized the usual cleaning tasks associated with each space into categories based on time and surface. In doing so, you'll be able to determine what you can do in the time you have. Each set of times, tasks, and surfaces gets your space ready for guests.

It's easy to find yourself in a situation where even with a whole day's notice, there's only a short amount of time available to clean. The rest of your schedule demands attention leaving you stressed about visiting guests. In this section, I break down cleaning tasks in your kitchen by the time it takes to do them. Even if you only have 10 minutes to spare, you can make an impact in your space. Pick and choose each cleaning task based not only on the time you have available, but your immediate needs. If your sink is empty, but your counters cluttered, then tackle the clutter. There are multiple tasks in each category allowing you to mix different tasks together to equal the amount of time you have. If you have half an hour of time, you can complete both a 10 minute cleaning task *and* a 20 minute cleaning task.

10 Minute Clean

Clear counters: Putting food away, clearing trash, and moving dishes to the sink can give you a clear line of sight around the kitchen before you even pick up a cleaning cloth. If you do have time leftover, you can wipe down the counters.

Wipe down appliances: Starting with the larger appliances like ranges, dishwashers, and refrigerators, wipe down appliance fronts with a soft cloth and your favorite cleaner. If you have more time, move on to smaller appliances like blenders, toasters, and microwaves.

20 Minute Clean

Unload and load the dishwasher and/or dishrack: Clearing out your sink gives an instant boost to the look of your kitchen. It not only declutters dishes, but cleans them.

Bonus time: Keep your favorite sink cleaner close at hand so you can clean the sink.

Sweep and mop floors: A broom is easier to set up than a vacuum, so grab it out of the closet and start sweeping. When finished, tackle any spots on the floor before using a dry mop with your favorite cleaner to mop the area.

30 Minute Clean

Clear the counters: With half an hour, you can tackle everything on your counter. Move dishes to the sink and trash to the receptacle. Working clockwise, wipe down counters around the kitchen. Empty the countertop dish rack, if you have one. Take any clutter found and put it away where it belongs, even if it lives in a different room.

Clean inside appliances: Tackle the crumbs and food residue buildup in all your small appliances. Clean out your toaster oven, microwave, bread toaster, coffee maker, and anything else that collects crumbs. If you have more time, wipe down any other small appliance that could use an exterior clean. Blenders, hand mixers, and any other countertop appliances can pick up food residue during meal prep or clean up.

Building a Cleaning Schedule

This section breaks down even more cleaning tasks, including deep cleaning, to provide you the pieces you need to put together a cleaning schedule. Part of a successful cleaning schedule and the trick I use to keep my own home clean involves doing a little bit each day. In this kitchen chapter, as well as the chapters on other rooms, I've defined cleaning times for the most common tasks. Using that knowledge, you can build your weekly and even monthly cleaning schedule. Some tasks, like cleaning out the fridge, should be done once a month or every other week. Other tasks, like vacuuming floors, should be done more frequently. Start with the time you're allowing for cleaning your home each day, whether it's an hour or 30 minutes, and build these tasks in with the ones for other rooms. This chapter and the next few are like a buffet of options meant to help you find what works best for your home.

This section will also give you the best methods for cleaning everything from garbage cans to stovetops. Each method was developed to save time and strain, making cleaning a breeze.

Appliances

Countertop appliances (30 minutes): Tackle the crumbs and food residue buildup in all your small appliances. Clean out your toaster oven, microwave, bread toaster, coffee maker, and anything else that collects crumbs. Wipe down the exterior. Blenders, hand mixers, and any other countertop appliances can pick up food residue during meal prep or clean up. Wipe their exteriors and remove all grease and food spots.

Refrigerator (1 hour): Start by clearing out old or expired food. Empty food storage containers and stack them next to the sink. Once the fridge contents have been pared down, start from the top of the fridge and work your way down removing each shelf to wash it in the sink. Use soap and water. As you work your way down from the top of the fridge, use a cloth wet with hot water to tackle food stains. Then take your favorite disinfecting cleaner and clean each area of the fridge. Next, turn your focus to the exterior. If the exterior is cluttered with papers and magnets, remove them all. Go through and get rid of any that are out of date or no longer useful. While the magnets are off, find your favorite all-purpose cleaner and wipe down the exterior, including the handles and the gaskets. The gaskets are the rubber material used to frame the door and ensure an airtight seal when the fridge and freezer sections are closed.

Tip: refrigerator handles should be cleaned weekly to cut down on germs, while a deeper cleaning can be done once a month.

Stove (2-12 hours): You can follow the directions on a store bought oven cleaner to tackle the mess from overflowing dishes. You can also use the Ultimate Non-Abrasive Disinfecting Oven Cleaner from chapter 3 to take on any messes in your oven and see it shine again. If you're deep cleaning your oven on a regular basis, say once a month, it's good to let the oven cleaner recipe sit overnight on the food buildup. The next day you can clean it up while also wiping down the oven walls. To keep food from building up in your oven between deep cleanings, set a timer for 30 minutes after a spill to allow the oven to cool. Once the temperature of the oven walls is lowered enough that you can wipe the surface safely, wet a cloth and clean up the mess. Tackling the biggest part of a food spill in an oven will keep spills from heating and smoking during future cooking cycles.

Dishwasher (1 hour): The actual time cleaning the dishwasher is probably 10 minutes, but involves running the dishwasher for a cycle in the middle. Start out by checking the trap for any food pieces that did not dissolve during wash cycles. Fill the detergent reservoir with white vinegar and run it through a cycle, but leave out the drying part at the end to save a little energy. When completed, sprinkle borax in the bottom and with a soft brush or cloth, wipe down the walls of the dishwasher.

Behind appliances (30 minutes): Take care of the spaces behind appliances to keep odors from food messes and air allergens down. For the oven, carefully slide away from the wall. If you're not sure of the floor's scratch resistance, use cut up rags to slide under the front feet of the oven. Use a second person to push up on the oven to be able to slide the rags under the feet. If you have a gas stove, be mindful of the connection and don't overextend it by moving your range out too far. Once you have moved the stove a safe distance back from the wall, use a vacuum with a scrap of pantyhose covering the end to pick up large items. Remove the scrap and then vacuum the rest. Using a dry mop, mop the area behind the stove. If you are able to move the stove completely out, you'll be able to get more of the floor. This method is for open space you're able to create behind the appliance for cleaning.

For your fridge, carefully slide it away from the wall. Avoid jostling or tipping to prevent the coolant inside from moving around too much and ending up in the wrong components. You should be able to remove it completely from the wall accessing the full square footage it occupies when in place. If not, defer to the oven instructions for careful cleaning of the area you can access. For cleaning the full area, use a vacuum or broom to collect any dust or dirt. Use your favorite floor cleaner to wipe down the floor. Use your favorite duster to dust the walls surrounding the fridge.

Floors and Windows

Vacuum or Sweep (15 minutes): Depending on your equipment and floor size, it may be faster to use a broom and sweep. Vacuums can be faster, depending on how easily accessible it is. Either way, this task takes about 15 minutes or less.

Dry mop (15 minutes): Dry mopping is the fastest way to get the deep set dirt off the floor. Use a Bona® or off-brand alternative mop system that includes washable pads and a broom-length handle. It doesn't take a lot of storage and can be accessed quickly. Use it with your favorite floor cleaner in a spray bottle avoiding the lengthy drying times of wet mopping.

Windows (10 minutes): Take your favorite window cleaner, homemade or store bought, and lightly spray all your windows. Let them set as you work your way through the panes of all your kitchen windows. Take a soft cloth and wipe in a circular motion.

Deep Cleaning

Trash receptacle (15 minutes): You may have a simple plastic can that sits under the sink or a plastic liner inside of a can with a lid. If you have more than just the standalone plastic can, add about 5 more minutes to the deep cleaning time. Start by removing any leftover garbage pieces from the bin. Then, using your favorite disinfectant spray, spritz the inside of the bin and let sit. Turn on the hot water in your kitchen sink and prop up the bin on one side of the sink. Wash the inside with your cleaning brush (not the one used on dishes) and dish soap. To clean the outside, spritz with your favorite disinfectant cleaner and wipe down with a soft cloth to dry. Once dry, sprinkle some baking soda in the bottom of the bin to help soak up odors and fight moisture.

Sink faucet (10 minutes): This area of your kitchen can become especially grimy and water-stained after heavy use. To restore the shine, take your favorite cleaner with degreasing power and cover the faucet. Use one that is thick and coats the surface. Wait two minutes and start wiping the faucet with a soft cloth. Work slowly ensuring each spot has been reached. If there is any cleaning residue leftover, take a clean damp cloth and wipe down the faucet. Polish with a clean dry cloth to remove any further moisture.

Cabinet faces (1-4 hours): The time it takes for this task is dependent on how many cabinets are in your kitchen. In a large kitchen with both upper and lower cabinets throughout, 4 hours will be a correct estimation of time. With a stack of soft cloths and a good wood cabinet polishing solution (like Wood Magic Furniture Cleaner and Polish®), work your way clockwise on the upper cabinets. Open doors and drawers to reach areas hidden when doors are closed. Move on to the lower cabinets working in the same clockwise direction. Cleaning and polishing will not only remove grease and food residue, but leave a protective barrier and sheen behind.

Butcher blocks (15 minutes): Invest in a good wax-and-oil product and using a soft cloth, apply to your butcher block. Wait 20 minutes and wipe off excess. You should perform this each time the wind starts to dry out.

Countertops (1 hour): You may be able to complete this in less than an hour depending on the surface area of your counters, but an hour is typical for this multi-step deep clean. After clearing the counter of any items, begin by dispensing a gentle dish soap on the counter. Wet a soft cloth in warm water and begin cleaning the counter in a circular motion. Use a razor (stone and granite counters) or a plastic tool (composite or other hard surface counters) to remove any stuck on food. Rinse your soft cloth in warm water to begin wiping away the soap mess. After your counter is free of soap and excess water, wipe down with a dry cloth. If you have stone counters, including granite, take your favorite stone-safe disinfectant and spray onto counters. Wipe with a clean cloth. Using your favorite polish safe for your counter surface, apply to counters with a soft cloth for an even better sheen.

These deep cleaning techniques are done on a rotating basis in my home. Rather than adhering to a schedule tied to time, I employ them on the basis of use. If I have a weekend of hosting guests with all the meals to go with, I'll spend time starting Monday through the rest of the week taking on one task at a time. You don't want to spend the following weekend cleaning up from the previous, so take chunks of time during your week to complete important deep cleaning tasks.

Many people think the only way you can have a clean and presentable kitchen is by putting in multiple hours deep cleaning every surface. Thankfully, the truth is a lot more simple. By breaking up kitchen tasks into routine cleaning and deep cleaning, you can have a guest-ready kitchen at a moment's notice. Even when life gets in the way of your regular routine, there are simple ways to tidy up quickly. Use the kitchen advantage of multitasking to stay motivated. The results are rewarding for both you and your guests.

Chapter 6: Living Areas

The number of uses for a living space, including the traditionally titled living room, is expansive. This space can be solely dedicated to proper seating to support socializing when guests are over. It can also shift shape depending on the needs of the day. Seating for a large group can give way to workspace for a large hands-on project. Keeping the space clean and ready for your next project or visit from houseguests requires a few thoughtful strategies. The pressure points in a living area will differ from every other room in the home. This chapter will identify those points and provide effective solutions to taking the pressure off them.

Three pressure points of a living room:

Dust: Dust is composed of many ingredients from your environment. It is the collection of your hair, skin cells, fur from pets, dirt, and so much more. The amount of dust that collects will depend on your environment. A home with pets will have more dust building up faster than homes without pets. A home with 6 people living in it will have more dust than a home with just one person.

To get ahead of the dust in your home, there are 2 things you can do right now. The first is to ensure all your air filters are changed on a regular basis. The general rule is that the thicker the filter, the longer it can go without changing. Some filters need to be changed monthly while others last up to 6 months. Determine the rating on your filters and schedule their replacement accordingly. No matter what the filter manufacturer recommends, you'll need to also assess your home in deciding when to replace filters. With multiple pets and people, your air filter may need to be changed out more often.

The second thing applies to households with pets. If you have cats and dogs, it's important to brush them on a regular basis. A weekly brushing with a Furminator® or similar brush will remove excess fur not only from the top coat, but the layer beneath. If it's difficult to keep your pet still for a long period of time to brush them, keep a small brush close at hand and perform the task in short increments throughout the week.

In terms of dusting tools, invest in a microfiber duster that not only attracts dust as it moves over surfaces, but can be washed after use. This saves you money over time by foregoing frequent purchases of disposable cloths. It also means you don't run out of cloths requiring you to go to the store just to get your cleaning finished. If you have a ceiling fan in your living area, an extendable tool with a special attachment is worth purchasing. This tool is made to glide over each fan blade capturing dust and making the job quick. I say it's worth investing in because of the time saved over a traditional method of bringing out a step-ladder and wiping each blade down by hand.

For objects on surfaces, dust them before dusting surfaces. Just as you want to dust your home from top to bottom (if you have multiple levels), you want to dust your objects and surfaces in the same way. This will keep dust falling to each successive level rather than stirring it up to sit on a surface you already dusted.

Clutter: One of the best ways you can stay on top of clutter is by designating a home for everything in it. There will be activities that always take place in the living area, like board games and movie watching. Find storage solutions for the objects that support those activities. For activities that are done in multiple parts of the home, like laundry folding, letter writing, even grocery list writing, keep surfaces clear to allow yourself space for these items. By giving everything that resides in the living area a home, you're clearing space on surfaces for those temporary items to stay while in use. By designating a spot for each object, you'll be able to easily tidy up before you even leave the room.

The living area is one room where a 5 minute decluttering session should be done daily. With its many uses, it's inevitable that by the end of the day, there's more mess than in other rooms. Taking a few minutes to return items to the rooms they belong will cut down on the overall clutter in the space. This makes it easy to focus on cleaning for impending guests and to meet your own cleaning schedule.

Floors: Floors in the living area are subject to every kind of dirt and dust buildup from supporting the life that happens within. There are a few ways you can get ahead of that dirt and dust while lessening the burden of cleaning the floors. Start with your entryway. Implement a shoe storage and organization system that will cut down on dirt in the rest of your home by trapping it near the door. Use a low pile rug in the entry to capture small particles of dirt.

Even with diligence at the front door, the living area can quickly collect dirt, dust, and hair tracked in from across the house. Carpet is an easy way to obscure dirt until you can vacuum, but hard flooring like wood or vinyl can be easier to clean when spills happen. A happy medium is a hard flooring with an area rug or two. The rugs will help capture all the dust, dirt, and hair to keep the floor cleaner between vacuuming. If drinks spill on the rug, you can spot clean. If the spot is beyond the cleaners you have at home, it should be taken in to be cleaned professionally.

I recommend rugs even if you are working with a carpeted area. Tastefully selected runners and other area rugs can help cut down on deep stains on your carpet from spills or high traffic. They can even be useful when needing to conceal stains you've spot cleaned, but will need to deep clean with a professional machine. This is especially important in a vacation rental living space. If you're experiencing a high volume of guests, there may not be enough time to professionally clean your carpet after a guest spills something. In a case where you must check in another guest before tending to the carpet, rugs offer a quick temporary solution. This will help keep your guests pleased with the appearance of your space without the need to alter reservations to do so. Always spot clean any carpet before a new guest arrives. If you make it the first on your cleaning list for turning over the space, there will be ample time to see if it is effective.

As for cleaning floors, make the most of your time by starting in one high traffic spot and working your way into the room going from one side of the other and back. Vacuuming or sweeping this way is similar to the difference between the two popular brands of robotic vacuums found in homes today. The Shark® brand robotic vacuum programs a pattern into a robot that operates until it reaches an obstacle before turning another direction. The final pattern looks something like the pattern of a 1990's screensaver where the software logo bounced around the screen. The iRobot Roomba® robotic vacuum performs its function in a simple up and down pattern. If the tray fills up halfway through a room, you know exactly where it stops. Similar with your vacuuming and sweeping, if you're called away in the middle of your work, you know exactly where you left off when you utilize an up and down pattern.

Speaking of robotic vacuums, I do appreciate their utility and would recommend them to certain households. They are an expensive cleaning tool, especially since they cannot completely replace your old vacuum. You will still need something to be able to grab quickly to clean when there is a time crunch. The cycle of the robotic vacuum often requires more time than you have (especially if you're pressed for it). I suggest this as an optional tool, as opposed to a must-have. In addition, the point of this book is not about filling your cleaning closet with expensive gadgets, but helping you keep your house cleaning under control.

Cleaning For Unexpected Guests (15 min):

When unexpected guests are en route, the part of your living area that probably scares you the most is the clutter. This includes snacks left out after watching a movie the night before, opened mail piling up and laundry waiting to be folded. All of this can be handled swiftly to allow yourself a few minutes to sweep or vacuum the floor.

Start with paper: Walk around the living space and gather all of the paper in sight. This includes magazines, mail, flyers and everything that is flat. Stack all paper neatly together in a corner of the room. If you really don't want any of it out, you can relocate it to another room temporarily. However, that often leads to important papers being lost and lessens the chance of you dealing with the stack when guests leave.

Organize the clutter: Perhaps you were doing a home manicure and left all your tools out. Maybe you had your camera and its cleaning kit out to perform maintenance. Whatever clutter you have left out on surfaces, arrange it so it looks like it belongs there. The aesthetic difference between a camera cleaning kit being strewn onto a coffee table and pieces of the same kit laid out in perfect symmetry is quite enormous. Like with paper, it's important to keep these items close at hand in the space. Taking part in the system of stacking clutter away behind closed doors does little to help your overall goal of a cleaner and more tidy home.

Take care of the trash: Since living areas are for meant for living, trash is inevitable. Take the snack wrapper left behind and the junk mail piled on the side table to their proper home. Glance next to and behind furniture for any trash you may have missed.

Focus on the floors: Dust on surfaces is a byproduct of living that doesn't pronounce itself as loudly as dirt on floors. In an effort to have the greatest impact on a living space in a short period of time, focus on the floors. If the vacuum doesn't stand a chance of getting taken out and put away in time, grab the broom and sweep. If you have carpet and thus need the vacuum, focus on high traffic areas first before moving to other parts of the room.

Whether announced or forgotten about, guests will first take notice of the aesthetic organization of your living space. They are not going to be concerned with why you didn't put your manicure kit away or why they must look at a stack of paper. They're going to see the clean lines and organization first and foremost. While the empty space of coffee and side tables may present a spotless image, they can't spark conversation like the contents of your letter writing kit or the tools for cleaning a camera.

Embrace the fact that your life cannot be completely concealed. It is your home after all, the space in which you live a good part of your life. At the end of the day, guests are here for you, not a spotless space that fell out of a magazine.

Clean by surface:

Upholstery: Upholstery fabric found on furniture and even throw pillows is woven to withstand much more than the clothes fabric. The newest upholstered furniture even mixes in technology to boost the life and durability of its fabric. Many upholstered fabrics contain threads and compounds to block water, similar to a raincoat. There are fabrics whose dyes are meant to withstand years of spot cleaning without losing their complexion. When it comes to cleaning upholstery, it's important to first arm yourself with knowledge about the fabric.

Most upholstery fabrics will be able to withstand the chemicals from a spot cleaner. Nevertheless, make sure you test a small inconspicuous area with the product before using on the rest of the upholstery. Fabrics like silk and velvet require additional caution and should be cleaned by professionals. For fabrics made of cotton and synthetics, a store bought stain remover from a brand like Woolite® will be engineered to safely remove stains. Use a soft cloth and follow the directions on the bottle.

If you're looking to simply spruce up your upholstery rather than tackle a specific stain, a simple fabric spray can be used. Fill a spray bottle with 1 cup white vinegar and 3 cups water. Mist over the upholstery without soaking it. The vinegar will lift scents left behind by removing them from the upholstery.

If the lifestyle in your home involves pets and children, consider investing in upholstered furniture with removable covers. Stylish and beautiful furniture can also be easy to keep clean when it utilizes removable covers. Machine wash these fabrics according to their label.

Furniture: To help prevent furniture from getting dirty, you can implement a few items into your lifestyle. Coasters for drinks are helpful for wood furniture as well as furniture made of other materials. Custom cut glass tops can also prolong the surface of furniture, wooden or otherwise. Even without custom glass, you can utilize textiles appropriate to your decor to act as a protective layer between furniture and spills.

For cleaning all furniture and making it last, take a damp cloth and wipe down tops, sides, legs, and feet. By running over every inch of your furniture with this soft cloth, you're able to capture all of the dirt and dust built up. For everyday cleaning of wood furniture, use only a soft cloth. You can boost the shine of the wood with wax cleaners, but they leave a film behind. After the film accumulates, the initial purpose of the wax cleaner is lost on the build-up.

Living areas are often the most used rooms in homes and the most visible to guests. Their importance can inspire you to focus more on the decor in a living room than other rooms in your home. Consider looking at your decor from the perspective of cleaning, rather than strictly expressing your own style. Ask yourself what could be moved or eliminated completely to cut down on your cleaning time. You may forego placing any decorative items on the floor to speed up the floor cleaning process. Perhaps you decide to express your style in larger objects rather than smaller ones because they're easier to dust. It's easy to meld your taste with an easy to clean living area.

This chapter empowers you with the knowledge and techniques to create and maintain a clean space in your living area. This is hugely impactful on your state of mind and well-being because living areas are often the first space you see when arriving home. They can also hold so much meaning due to their role as a setting for our lives. Living areas host parties with friends, quiet solitude with a good book, and much more. Keeping it clean may offer a positive impression to visiting guests, but it can have the most impact on you and the life you bring to it.

Chapter 7: Bedrooms

Bedrooms are a sanctuary within the home where rest and relaxation should take precedence. If you live in a studio apartment, your bedroom may also be part of the living and dining area. If you have roommates, you may keep a TV in your room to allow for separate relaxation. It may be the only space for your home office and thus needs to be supportive of your working mind (not to mention, your resting mind). Even if you only use your bedroom for sleep, you're spending a large amount of time in one room of your home. Cleaning and keeping it that way is supportive of your entire day. Getting the best sleep in a clean environment, powers your entire day.

As important as a clean bedroom is to your life, it can be easy for your schedule to get in the way and cause you to shut the door on the mess. When that happens, use the cleaning tasks and times below to help get you back on track. They're perfect for maintaining a clean bedroom in the time available to you. The following increments and tasks can be combined with other house cleaning tasks to be most efficient.

10 minutes:

Make bed: One of the fastest ways to improve the look of your bedroom is by making your bed. If you have a second set of bed linens, there's even time to switch everything out in less than 10 minutes. If there's anything on the bed prior to making it up, take a minute to put everything away in its proper place.

Fold laundry: If the state of your bed is less unkempt and more covered in fresh laundry, sit down and take 10 minutes to fold and put it away. Setting a timer for 10 minutes and committing to folding and putting it away is the perfect solution for the multi-step process of clothes laundering.

20 minutes:

Vacuum floors: Pick up any clutter and vacuum every inch of the floor. If you have area rugs, shake them out or put them in the washer to start a cycle. If there's time leftover, deal with the clutter you picked up by returning it to its home, wherever in the house that may be.

Remove clutter: Starting from the top and working your way down, clear all your surfaces of clutter. If you don't have time to put everything away, at least arrange everything neatly so that the aesthetic comprises clean lines rather than disjointed piles of objects. Give special attention to your nightstand to ensure its continued functionality for you.

30 minutes:

Wipe down surfaces: In 30 minutes, you can wipe down all surfaces and sides. Starting with the tallest piece of furniture, take a damp cloth and wipe down the top before moving to the sides and legs. Move on to shorter pieces, like nightstands or headboards. Don't forget about mirrors or windows. Clear up the reflective surface on both with a soft cloth and a bit of window cleaner.

Return items: Gather the items around your bedroom that belong elsewhere in your home. Take the time to put them precisely where they belong, not just anywhere in the room they reside. Taking time to do this not only declutters your bedroom, but helps support the overall cleanliness of your home.

The following check points need special attention in the bedroom, even if you neglect them in other parts of your home. They all directly affect the quality of your sleep and overall liveability of the room.

Clean air:

Clean air is vital to the place where you spend so much of your time. Investing in an air purifier will ensure the air you breathe during every REM cycle is clean. You can modify your existing HVAC system to include various types of filters that work differently from the standard filters. This will affect the air throughout your home rather than just your bedroom. Because these modifications can be more costly than purchasing a one-room purifier, they require more financial planning to achieve. For now, a standalone air purifier will achieve the desired result.

In order to remove mold, allergens and other pollutants from your air, you would need multiple types of air purifiers (and even a dehumidifier) running at the same time. The maintenance alone for all of these machines could take up a half-day of cleaning time. The best solution is to identify the needs unique to your health and your space. Different types of air purifier filters are good at pulling different things out of the air.

Types of air purifier filters:

HEPA filters: High Efficiency Particulate Air or HEPA is a type of filter meant to pull dust and other allergens out of the air. It can catch particulates of varying sizes and is completely sealed, meaning those particulates won't escape again. You will need to replace the filter on a regular basis, as it cannot be cleaned and reused.

Ionizer: Ionizer purifiers work by sending out negative ions into your space that latch onto positively charged ions, which includes allergens, dust and bacteria. These particles are then trapped by the purifier.

Most air purifiers that have an ionizer also have a HEPA filter to help filter more out of the air. The effectiveness of the ionizer will depend on how frequently you dust and vacuum. Since the negative ions going out don't always make it back through the filter, they end up on positively charged surfaces in the room and floor. This is acceptable if you vacuum and dust on a regular basis, but something to be mindful of.

UV filters: UV light can attract bacteria and mold in the air trapping it. Unfortunately, in order to be effective they draw on more power and can't trap the UV-resistant bacteria in the air.

An air purifier with a HEPA filter provides a happy medium wherein dust and particles are trapped while maintaining the machine is as simple as replacing a filter. If your bedroom is subject to mold because of the climate you're in or the placement of the room in your home, consider investing in a dehumidifier that allows you to control the humidity. You can keep the humidity at a comfortable level without spurring on mold growth in your space.

Other ways to keep your air clean include dusting, regular bedding changes, and preventing dirt from entering your room. You should dust your bedroom every week, even if dusting in other rooms falls out of your schedule.

You should also change your bedding at least once a week. Showering before bed can help cut down on dust and allergens that build up in your bedding over the course of a week. If you have curtains in your bedroom, launder them regularly, about once a month. If the fabric is not machine washable, use your dust attachment for your vacuum to clean them once a month.

Clean aesthetics:

One way to help support a cleaner environment in your bedroom is by removing unnecessary clutter from view. Put aside the bottles of perfume, pieces of jewelry, and other accessories as forms of decor. Instead, opt for pieces that fit into the design of your bedroom space and reflect you. To keep the useful items close at hand, utilize the storage already found in the room, dresser drawers and shelves.

Due to the proximity of your bedroom to the bathroom, you may find yourself surrounded by piles of clean and dirty laundry. Luckily, there is a simple solution to eliminating the clutter. Find decorative baskets that can hold clean laundry before you've had a chance to fold it and put it away. Keep a second basket for dirty clothes to keep your bedroom clutter down. It's easy to transfer the dirty clothes from the decorative basket to the laundry basket. This process allows you to quickly sort your laundry on the spot. Look for decorative baskets with handles that provide portability and find a style that includes a lid for additional concealment.

Hidden spaces:

It's often the hidden spaces that contain the most dirt and dust in your bedroom. Furniture like dressers and beds often are designed with decorative legs raising them off the floor. The aesthetic is a pleasing one, but it means you'll need to be diligent about vacuuming under these pieces regularly. Even carpeted bedrooms have a buildup of dirt under furniture. Use vacuum attachments to reach as much as you can under furniture during routine vacuuming. If some spaces still prove difficult to reach, arrange to move furniture every few months to vacuum.

It's easy to shut the door to your bedroom and focus on the cleanliness in the rest of your home. In doing so, you end up neglecting one of the most sacred rooms. Your bedroom is a sanctuary, a place where you can rest and recharge. If you can keep its use to these purposes, you'll have a space that's easy to care for and keep clean.

Chapter 8: Bathrooms

The bathrooms in your home are some of the most important spaces to keep clean. Due to the nature of their use, they often contain more germs and bacteria than other spaces in your house. It's important to establish a cleaning routine for the bathroom that you can keep up with, even when life gets busy. To help you reset to a base level of clean, I've put together a number of different cleaning tasks organized by the time it takes to complete them. When it's the end of a long day and tomorrow is looking busier, you can pull out a task or two and take care of them immediately. This puts you in a cleaner position as you take on the remaining tasks the following day.

10 minutes:

Clear surfaces: Remove any clutter from countertops, shelves, and other surfaces. Return toiletries to where they belong and throw any trash away. Pick up any dirty laundry from the floor.

Wipe everything down: If clutter is not your obstacle, but dried toothpaste in the sink basin has you blocked, take 10 minutes and wipe everything down, including mirrors. Using a soft cloth and an all-purpose cleaner safe for your bathroom surfaces, wipe down the faucet, sink, and countertops. Then move on to the back of the toilet, the toilet seat, and the top of the toilet bowl. If there's time left over, take out your bathroom trash and replace the bag so it's ready for guests.

20 minutes:

Floors: Put your bath mats in the laundry and clear the floor of anything else before vacuuming or sweeping. Dry mop for an even deeper clean before laying out your cleaned bath mats.

Focus on sinks and toilets: By focusing on making the sinks and toilet shine in your bathroom, you're creating a focal point of clean for guests. Start with the toilet. Using your favorite disinfecting cleaner and a soft cloth, wipe down the toilet from top to bottom. Make sure you wipe down the entire outside of the toilet basin and get into the tight corners of the toilet's base. Gather your deep cleaning tools and finish at the sink. These tools include a toothbrush or similarly sized cleaning brush, your favorite sink cleaner, and a soft cloth.

Spray the faucet with the cleaner and let sit while you wipe the basin. Taking your toothbrush, scrub the faucet to remove any water spots, soap buildup, and other grime dulling the shine.

30 Minutes:

Focus on fixtures: Dusting a towel bar isn't the first thing that comes to mind when cleaning the bathroom, but it can be an important task in achieving a high standard of clean. Take account of all the fixtures in your bathroom, including any visible storage like decorative baskets or art hanging on the wall. Starting with the fixtures that are highest up, wipe down everything with a soft damp cloth. For items like decorative baskets, empty their contents, then hold the basket upside down over a trash can and brush out any dirt in the bottom with a dry toothbrush. For any bathroom art, assess the material and then use either a dry duster or a soft damp cloth to clean it. Replace any towels that were on towel bars and use this time to also put away any clothes hanging on bathroom hooks.

45 minutes:

Grout cleaning: Using a paste of bleach and baking soda, layer the lines of grout with cleaner. You can also use a store bought grout cleaner for this task.

Wait 15 minutes before returning with a toothbrush or similarly sized cleaning brush to scrub at each line of grout. Rinse with a wet damp cloth, making sure to rinse out the cloth regularly. Use your favorite tile cleaner on the entire surface of tile and grout to give it a polished look. A shower itself could take about 45 minutes, so decide if you're going to focus on the floor grout or shower grout.

If you have more than one bathroom, and you don't have a lot of time, mix and match the tasks above to achieve the same look in each bathroom.

If you have 30 minutes and 3 bathrooms, employ the decluttering cleaning task to bring them up to the same level of clean.

Daily bathroom habits:

Between bouts of cleaning, there are daily habits you can adopt to help support a guest-ready bathroom at all times. As with any new habit, it will take time to build them into your routine. I recommend starting with one habit for a week to feel the difference in your space. As that habit begins to establish itself in your routine, add another.

Habit #1: Pick up clothes

It's easy to let clothes pile up just outside the shower. It seems especially easy right after cleaning the bathroom when the floors are so fresh and sanitized. Make a point of getting any clothes that come off your body right into your hamper. If your bathroom is too small to keep a hamper, consider a small basket that can either hang on the towel rack or sit neatly under the sink to catch the day's clothes. Whichever way you choose, make sure it lessens the burden of putting clothes away and doesn't complicate it.

Habit #2: Find homes for products

As you integrate new products into your daily care routine, you should also incorporate a place for them to live. If your shower is separate from the rest of your bathroom, you might consider keeping lotion and face moisturizer within your shower to maximize counter space. If you tend to do your makeup in your bedroom, but lack storage, you might opt to keep products organized in a bathroom drawer. The products that can be left out should be the ones used on a daily or twice daily basis. Toothbrushes, hair brushes, makeup, shaving products, and facial creams all fall into this category. Choose what you'd like to keep out based on the size of the countertop or storage surface available. If you have a pedestal sink with barely enough room to hold a soap pump, consider a medicine cabinet or over-the-toilet shelving system. Both of these storage solutions will allow you to keep important products close at hand. If you have a large countertop surface surrounding your sink, consider decorative trays to separate sets of products from each other. Keeping them on trays means when it's time to clean, you can pick up the tray, move it, clean the area, and return the tray to its proper home.

With these tips in mind, it is also important to know when your storage is inefficient. If you find your daily routine is interrupted to retrieve a product, then it's being stored in the wrong place.

Habit #3: Use it and store it

When you've found homes for everything, this habit should be easy to adopt. When you use products during your morning and evening routines, return them back to where they belong. The few seconds it takes to open a drawer or cabinet door will save you several minutes when it comes time to clean the bathroom. If your products have packaging to be thrown away after use, make sure there is a trash can nearby.

The Perfect Guest Bathroom:

For guests, you may have a separate powder room with just a toilet and sink. Or perhaps your own bathroom may serve as the defacto guest bathroom. Whatever the case, there are a few simple ways to stock your bathroom so it is always ready for guests. Stock your toilet area with a surface cleaner or air spray guests can easily access if they need to utilize it. For menstruating guest, keep tampons and pads stocked and in plain sight. If you're stocking a bathroom for overnight guests, arrange containers of important tools like cotton balls and cotton tips for easy access. Always keep fresh hand towels and rolls of toilet paper in the bathroom, concealed in a decorative basket or stored under the sink.

Return to Factory Settings Clean:

This section is especially helpful when moving into a new place where "deep clean" was not part of the previous resident's vocabulary. It will also be useful when you wake up one day and realize how much of your daily routine has built up around faucets and drains. Deep cleans like the ones below can be done on an as needed basis. It will depend on the frequency of use the bathroom receives and can't always be scheduled. I recommend completing them as part of your entry into a new era of clean in your home.

Sink:

The pressure points in a sink tend to be the drain itself and the area where the base of the faucet meets the sink. It's easy for soap and other gunk to build up in these places creating a film that's difficult to tackle. Using your favorite deep cleaner or a mix of baking soda with vinegar, apply the cleaner and let sit for 10 minutes. You should cover the drain and the base of the faucet completely with the cleaner. Scrub the areas with a toothbrush or cleaning brush. Next, focus on the faucet itself. Using your favorite all-purpose cleaner, spray the faucet liberally and scrub each corner with the toothbrush. Wipe the cleaner and mess away with a soft cloth and assess any leftover dirt or stains. Repeat the process, if necessary. To give your sink basin a fresh look, use a cleaner safe for the surface and spray liberally. Working in a circular motion with a soft cloth, clean the basin. Use a clean dry soft cloth at the end to polish it up and remove any leftover cleaner residue.

Toilet:

Start from the top and work your way to the bottom. Using your favorite cleaner with disinfectant, clean the top of the toilet tank and work your way down the sides. Be sure to get the lever used to engage flushing. Wipe down the toilet cover, the toilet seat, and the rim of the basin underneath the toilet seat. Remove the toilet seat entirely with a screwdriver or appropriate tool. Set the toilet seat hardware in a large bin soaking in hot water and soap. Using a new soft cloth, scrub the toilet where the seat attached removing any stains hidden by the hardware. Rinse the toilet seat hardware and, if needed, use a paper towel to clean them when the water isn't enough. Spray your disinfectant cleaner on all components after washing in the sink and let dry. Put the seat back on the toilet. Move on to the bottom of the toilet basin wiping with the disinfectant cleaner. Work your way into the base of the toilet and even reach into the small space between the back of the toilet and the wall.

Shower:

Two of the most common types of showers are acrylic and tile. Both have their advantages and both can get to the point where they need a deep clean. If you have an acrylic shower, the first tool you'll need is the Mr. Clean Magic Eraser® or a store brand version of it. Use the eraser to tackle soap scum around the base of the tub and any spots on the walls of the shower. After using the eraser, take your favorite shower cleaner and soak the walls and base. Let sit for five minutes before scrubbing with a brush. Rinse with water and use a squeegee to help dry the surface without leaving spots. If you have a tile shower, most likely with a porcelain or similar tub, find your favorite grout cleaner and apply it to all lines of the grout. While that sits, focus your attention onto the basin or tub. Using a bleach-based cleaner, spray the basin or tub liberally. Once the tub is coated, use a cleaning brush to scrub in a circular motion. Work your way around the tub until you've scrubbed every part. Moving back to the grout, test a small section with your toothbrush to see if the cleaner has sat long enough. If the grout is noticeably different, go ahead and scrub the rest of the grout lines. Rinse the tile and grout with water before spraying your favorite disinfectant cleaner. Use a squeegee on the tile and grout before moving back to the basin or tub. Rinse the tub with hot water before spraying disinfectant cleaner and wiping the tub down.

You want it to be almost completely dry to avoid water spots. At the end of these cleaning techniques, your drain and showerhead should have gotten a clean of their own. If there are still water spots or stains, take a cleaner that can handle calcium, lime, and rust like CLR® and spray these areas. Let sit and then wipe away.

The products used in the deep clean of your bathroom are strong and effective. This also means that they contain chemicals that you may not want to be exposed to on a daily basis. Once your bathroom is cleaned using these products, you will be able to keep ahead of water stains and deep grout stains with your regular cleaning routine. These products should stay on the shelf more than they are used, but are so helpful when the situation warrants it.

Keeping a clean bathroom starts with a few daily habits and ends with a solid cleaning routine. In the middle, there's room for a deep clean that restores the space to its original fresh out-of-the-box state. As with timed tasks for other rooms, you can mix and match the tasks in this chapter.

Mixing them together, you can create a cleaning spree to match available time and the rooms that need attention. Your bathroom can be not only the room in which you prepare yourself for the day but a room frequented by visiting guests. It's easy for the room to fulfill its purposes when cared for properly using the tools and strategies in this chapter.

Chapter 9: Floors

The flooring in your home can be one of the most costly parts of construction and renovation. Even if you didn't foot the bill for the current flooring in your home, the rent or purchase price paid for your house includes the quality of the flooring material. Different types of flooring require different techniques, products, and tools. While there is often crossover in tools and even cleaning products, each material has its own quirks. This chapter breaks down the top flooring materials offering tips and techniques to clean quickly and effectively. In this chapter you will learn that it is possible to a have guest-ready floor merely days after cleaning.

Tile:

Tile is a natural choice for bathrooms and kitchens. In homes with warmer climates, tile is often used throughout the house. The standard material in tiles is ceramic which is then glazed to achieve different finishes. Floor tile is often going to have a glaze with some texture to prevent it from becoming dangerous when wet. The grouts used with floor tile are most likely sanded grout. Unsanded grout is typically reserved for glass tile to prevent scratching the tile surface during application. Tile and grout is easy to maintain and makes spot cleaning a breeze.

The right cleaner for your tile: Most tiles are non-porous and can be cleaned using a homemade cleaner or a store bought cleaner made for tile. One exception is stone tiles such as travertine. Travertine will require a stone cleaner, which can be purchased from your local hardware store or cleaning aisle of you local big box store like Target or Wal-Mart.

Dry cleaning:

There's a number of tools available to keep tile floors clean and their effectiveness depends on the use for the room. For tile in the kitchen, the most effective dry cleaning tool is a broom. A broom will clean up food crumbs of any size while a vacuum may not be able to handle larger pieces of debris. Tile in living areas can benefit from a dust mop that you can easily glide around the room collecting dust and dirt. Any excess can be swept right into a dustpan. In the bathroom, a broom or vacuum will do. If tile dominates your home, a vacuum will be the fastest way to remove dirt and dust.

Spot cleaning: There will inevitably be spots that require more than a once over with a mop. Depending on the spot, you may need to take a cloth wet with hot water and let it sit over the spot to loosen it up. After a few minutes, you can wipe it away.

Wet cleaning: Mopping with a dry mop, like the kit from Bona or a similar one from janitorial supply companies, is the best way to clean tile. When you have a dry mopping kit with multiple pads, you can easily change out a dirty pad for a clean one as you go along. This keeps dirt and germs from spreading around during mopping. Another great tool for tile is a steam mop. It's a happy medium between a traditional mop and a dry mop. You can fill up the tank with water, turn it on, and while waiting for the steam to build up, sweep or vacuum the area of tile. Steam mops also come with reusable pads, so you can change them during cleaning as they get dirty. A dry mop has a much lower buy in compared to the steam mop, but the steam mop cleans floors with no chemicals needed.

Tile sealing:

If installed properly, your grout would have received an application of sealer to deflect stains and signs of heavy use. It is recommended that you seal grout once a year, depending on how much traffic the tile endures. Your local hardware store will offer the sealer you need and the bottle contains instructions for application. In order to prep grout for sealing, reach for a bleach and baking soda paste that can remove even the deepest stains. Once the grout is rinsed of any leftover baking soda and fully dry, the grout is ready for sealing.

Hardwood:

Hardwood is a classic look that can be purchased new or found hiding under carpet and even salvaged from old homes. Caring for wood properly begins with understanding the type of wood used in the flooring. Pine is often a popular choice and cost effective, but it is a soft wood that regular sealing in the form of polyurethane or similar can make up for. Pine has a beautiful look, but care should be taken to protect it from scratches and dents by using area rugs. You can also initiate a no-shoes rule for your pine floors.

Pine is one of the softest woods, but there are many durable types used in flooring. Bamboo, oak, maple, ash, and even mahogany all make up strong hardwood floors. With proper sealing, you can easily clean all types of wood with homemade or store bought cleaners.

Dry Cleaning (Dusting): A soft dry cloth is perfect for gathering dust and debris from your wood floor. If you have a dry mop system to clean your floors, it's easy to change those pads for a soft one to take care of dusting.

Dry Cleaning (Vacuuming): Vacuuming can be a quick way to get dirt off hardwood floors, especially when there's too much for a duster to handle. To keep your floors in top shape, make sure your vacuum has a soft brush attachment. This will not only glide over the floor without scratching, it will also pick up hair and other fine particles ensuring they're trapped.

Spot cleaning: When there's a few drops of coffee or the results of your cat's sensitive stomach resting on your hardwood floors, reach for your favorite hardwood cleaner. Spray a little onto the spot and then begin your dry mopping process. By the time you get to the spot, it will come up easily.

Wet cleaning: A dry mop kit works well for hardwood and allows you to have a system that works in rooms with tile in addition to hardwood. Use a favorite hardwood cleaner and change the pads regularly to keep from dragging dirt around the floor. If your hardwood is older and lacks the strong seal of newer hardwood, you may want to use a floor wax like Minwax® or Old English® brand floor wax. These products not only clean, but leave behind a layer of wax as protection for the floor.

Protecting floors: Even with proper sealing, hardwood is subject to damage from furniture, shoes, and accidents. Take care with a few preventative measures and ensure the longevity of your floors. All furniture resting on hardwood should be outfitted with soft furniture pads on the points of contact with the floor. If you have any houseplants resting on the wood floor, make sure they have trays under them to collect any excess water that drains out of the pot. If there is water or pet damage that goes undetected, even the best sealants can be compromised. If this happens, you may need your floor professionally patched. For reasons like these, it's important to hold onto any leftover materials after a floor install.

Laminate:

Laminate is becoming a popular choice for flooring in kitchens, bathrooms, living areas, and even bedrooms. The technology for laminate has advanced to where it can look like hardwood or even plank tile. It's highly durable and able to withstand heavy wear and tear in kitchens as well as living areas. The maintenance of laminate is easy and the price is more affordable than hardwood or tile. In the kitchen, it provides the perfect blend of hardwood and tile. It's soft like hardwood making it easier to stand on for long periods but has the durability of tile when a dish is dropped or shoes are worn on it.

Dry cleaning: With varying textures of laminate, a vacuum is the best tool for picking up dirt and debris. You can use a soft brush attachment on your vacuum like you would with hardwood. This makes it easier to go room to room with the same equipment if you have multiple floor types in your home. A vacuum will grab all dust and dirt out of laminate efficiently without worrying about leaving anything behind.

Spot cleaning: Even with its durability, laminate is not meant to withstand abrasive cleaners. Instead, rely on the dry mop pads to work on tough spots and get into every space of the laminate surface. When those won't work, a plastic bristle brush is perfect for getting rid of a spot ahead of mopping.

Wet cleaning: Dry mop systems come with pads, often made of microfiber or longer loomed cotton, that will pick up dirt easily from any texture of laminate. You can use a favorite homemade cleaner or buy one made for laminate. There are even cleaners safe for both laminate and hardwood, cutting down on the number of products you need if you have multiple floor types in your home.

Carpets:

The variety of carpet types available creates a multitude of approaches to cleaning for one floor type. Low-pile carpet typically does not hold onto dirt and dust as easily as high-pile carpet. There's carpet specifically made for high-traffic areas that is not only low-pile, but tightly loomed to prevent tears or snags as well as repel dirt. Carpet is often the obvious choice to add warmth to a room, such as finished basements and bedrooms.

Dry cleaning: Vacuuming is the easiest way to get your carpets clean. To make sure you're getting the most out of the time spent vacuuming carpet, there's a few things to check on the vacuum itself. Make sure the brush is not wound completely with fibers and hairs. If it is, take a pair of scissors to begin cutting off the mess in sections. Make sure there is a new bag or the canister is completely empty before vacuuming. You don't want to have to empty the canister halfway through vacuuming and any dirt left in it will impede the machine's ability to collect more dirt. Make sure the filters are cleaned or replaced on a regular basis. A clogged filter will affect the suction of the vacuum. Make sure you adjust the brush height to match your carpet. If you have low-pile carpet, adjust it to a lower setting so it sits closer to the carpet itself. If you have high-pile, adjust it up so it sits far enough above the fibers to capture all dirt and dust as the brush spins.

Spot cleaning: The approach will be determined by the type of spot to be tackled. If a pet has an accident, you're not only dealing with a surface spot but anything that has drifted to the pad or subfloor below. Test an inconspicuous area first, but apply white vinegar liberally to the urine or feces stain. Then, sprinkle baking soda liberally over the spot. Cover with a laundry basket or similar to keep from walking on it and let dry for a few days. For non-pet stains, it's easy to keep a store bought cleaner on hand and follow the directions to remove the stain. Remember that a stain is easier to remove when it is still wet, so as soon as it happens, grab the cleaner and take care of it.

Wet cleaning: Depending on the volume of traffic on your carpet, wet cleaning should be done sparingly. Once a year or every other year will work depending on the volume of traffic. Refer back to the recipes chapter for a homemade concentrate to use in professional carpet cleaners. Store bought is fine, too, but homemade will save a little money.

Other flooring types:

Marble: Marble is porous and thus susceptible to stains without proper protection. Use a marble specific cleaner and avoid letting the cleaner dry on the marble. Always wipe up the cleaner and use a soft microfiber cloth to avoid scratches to the marble.

Stone: The extent of stone flooring in your home may be the fireplace hearth, but some homes have stone as flooring in other parts, as well. Stone, like travertine tile, can be porous and care should be taken not to leave liquids resting on it to dry. Wiping it down with a vinegar cleaner will remove everyday dirt and dust. If needed, scrubbing with a plastic bristle brush can help break up tough dirt.

It's not often that a home will have just one type of flooring throughout. Rather than let the various needs of flooring types fill utility closets with tools and cleaners, invest in items that can perform multiple functions. A vacuuming and mopping system that can go from tile to hardwood and then to laminate will make the job go by much faster. Vacuums that can transform quickly into the perfect dirt buster on carpet before gently taking up dust on hard flooring make the job less stressful. There are ways to cut down on the dirt and dust entering your house, but at the end of the day, your floors play catchall for your entire home. Find the right tools for your home and the task of keeping floors clean will become easier and more enjoyable.

Chapter 10: Additional Areas

The preceding chapters covered the rooms that take up the most space in your home and thus require the most detail for cleaning and upkeep. In this chapter, I'm sharing the proven strategies to keeping all the other spaces in your home immaculate. Garages, entryways, laundry rooms, and closets fill in the space around your larger living areas. While some are used exclusively for storage, others see high-foot traffic and use on a daily basis. Maintaining each space will help support your efforts to keep the rest of your home clean. They might be able to provide a quick getaway for clutter when guests drop in last minute. They might keep all your cleaning products organized and tidy motivating you in your mission to keep house. Each space has a purpose and keeping it clean means it can fulfill that purpose to the fullest extent.

Closets:

Your home most likely has at least one clothes closet and one linen closet (while some homes have a separate coat closet and utility closet). Altogether, closets are the secret ingredients to keeping a home clean. Without them, clothes, shoes, linens, and more would be strewn everywhere or crammed into furniture wardrobes taking up extra space. Depending on the type of closet, there are a few strategies to keep these spaces clean.

Clothes closets: Whether you have a walk-in closet big enough to fit an area rug or a standard depth closet with a simple clothes bar, it can get messy quickly. Forgotten clothes fall back behind stored suitcases while the floor completely misses vacuuming because it's closed off and out of mind. With the fibers from clothes both dirty and clean, it's important to dust your closet from top to bottom on a regular basis. A microfiber duster works perfectly well and can fit around every ring of an open shelf.

Part of cleaning your clothes closet is decluttering. Having less in the space means less dust created and an easier time cleaning the space. When decluttering, make sure you have the adequate storage containers for what's in your closet. Proper storage solutions keep contents fresh and ready to use at a moment's notice. Plastic bins in varying sizes offer transparent views to see contents while baskets with lids let items breathe. Baskets are great for sweaters and clothes while bins hold books, sports equipment and travel accessories.

When decluttering and organizing your closet, keep the floor open as possible. This will ensure that when you are vacuuming the room just outside, you can quickly cover the closet floor by simply opening the doors. It's easy for dust and dirt to get trapped in closet floors, especially if they're carpet.

Linen closets: Linen closets can quickly become the messiest room in a house due to their contents and use of those items. Sheets and blankets fall to the floor when you try to grab a specific set. Floors can become covered in dust from the linens themselves. In order to keep the linen closet cleaner for longer, invest in storage that you can label. Store all linens categorically making it easy to find what you need.

If you have solid shelves, wipe them down with a soft cloth and and an all-purpose cleaner once a month. If you have wire shelves, a microfiber duster works well. Keep floors as open as possible to make it easy to vacuum or sweep. Many linen closets perform double-duty storing linens as well as cleaners and other tools. If this is the case in your closet, pay special attention to where you store each item. Cleaners should all be stored below linens. This prevents accidental spills onto fabrics and offers the floor to land on. If you have small children in the home and are worried about cleaners being in reach, invest in a child lock for the linen closet door. Utilize the space on the back of the linen closet door to store tools like brooms and dusters. Depending on the depth of the closet, you may also be able to fit a vacuum in the space as well.

Storage closets: If a home lacks a garage space, there is often a storage closet to make up for it. They're used to hold tools, sporting equipment, and anything else that isn't used in the home itself. This area should have its own set of tools for cleaning to keep outside dirt from being brought into the home. A stiff bristle broom for sweeping is a must. They can easily be found at your local hardware store (sometimes described as a shop or industrial broom).

If you have solid shelves in the storage area, keep them dust free by wiping them down with a wet soft cloth either monthly or bi-monthly. The frequency will depend on the season and how often the items in storage are being used and put back. Utilize plastic storage bins for items in this area to make them easier to clean when they collect dust.

Pantry closets: A pantry closet should be on your schedule when vacuuming the room surrounding it. As for cleaning, it's good to go through the pantry every 3 months and get rid of expired food. In doing so, you can also reorganize what you have making it easier to see what's available. Wipe shelves from top to bottom before sweeping the floor and mopping it with your dry mop system.

Laundry Room:

The most frequent cleaning need I've found in laundry rooms is dusting. The clothes dryer is almost always in use and the filter cleaned out between every load. This allows for many particulates to make their way into the air and settle onto surfaces. To help cut down on dust from the lint trap, keep a lidded trash can close to the dryer. When it comes to cleaning the rest of the laundry room, start with any exposed surfaces like shelves and the outside of your washer and dryer. Take time to clean out the lint trap using your vacuum hose. A full cleaning of the dryer duct should be conducted every 3 months or so, depending on the volume of usage.

To clean inside your washer, begin by cleaning out the washing machine filter. Depending on how full it is, there may be some water that leaks onto the ground when removing. Keep a towel close by just in case. Then, use the wash setting on your washer or fill the detergent dispenser with white vinegar. In newer washers, throw in a few towels so they are able to sense clothing, provide enough water and put them through a hot wash cycle. Once you've finished cleaning the rest of the room, vacuum or sweep the floor and mop. Wash or vacuum any area rugs used in the space before putting them back down.

Mudrooms and Entryways:

Mudrooms and entryways should contain many of the same tools to keep dirt from going further into your home. Mudrooms tend to be more concealed from the rest of your home while entryways bring you right into the heart of the house. In both settings, proper shoe storage will help keep dirt manageable. Find a system that allows for dirt to collect under where the shoes sit. A wire shelf with a tray underneath accomplishes this goal.

The shelves can be cleaned and dusted so that all dirt and debris is knocked onto the tray below it. The tray can then be dumped into the trash after collecting all the dirt. Find a machine washable rug to keep right at the entryway collecting dirt and dust. With several copies of a machine washable rug, you can change it out a few times a week keeping the area clean. Being able to change out the rug at a moment's notice is what keeps your home guest ready at all times.

Door handles and the doors themselves get a lot of wear and tear. Take care of scuffs from shoes with a Mr. Clean® Magic Eraser. Regularly wipe down the door handle and the area around it to keep dirt from building up and discoloring the area. You can also invest in a decorative toe kick to fit at the base of the door and take the brunt of accidental bumps with shoes and other items going in and out of the door.

Garage:

The main area of concern in a garage is the floor. Leaves, dirt, and trash can easily pile up all over the space. Using an industrial broom, also known as a shop broom, you can sweep the area quickly collecting dirt and trash. Keep a trash can in the garage to avoid temptation to leave it behind or track more dirt into the house looking for a receptacle. If you park your vehicle in the garage, use old cardboard to collect any leaking car fluids keeping the floor clean.

Outdoor Spaces:

Similar to the garage, outdoor spaces will be subject to the whims of mother nature when it comes to dirt buildup. There will also be more spiderwebs and insect homes competing for the space. Depending on whether your outdoor area is decking or a stone patio, there are different ways to keep it clean.

Decks: Wood and synthetic wood decks have several options for keeping the dirt and dust off. One tool to handle it all is a wide industrial broom that can reach between boards due to its weight and operation. There's no need to pick it up and sweep like a traditional broom. Simply set it on the surface and guide it from one end to the other until the entire area has been swept. Choosing this option means you'll need to move deck furniture as you sweep. If that's not feasible, consider an electric leaf blower. With less immediate air pollution than gas leaf blowers, an electric leaf blower can be quickly adjusted on the go. You can increase the power to remove tough piles of wet leaves or needles. You can decrease it as you dislodge dirt from under furniture.

Even with adjustable settings, there is risk of getting dirt on deck furniture cushions. It's safest to remove them before operating the leaf blower to keep them in shape. Water is also an effective tool for a deep clean of your deck but one that should be used sparingly to conserve the resource. Pressure washing is especially useful when preparing to re-stain a deck. Save the water method for instances like that and use one of the other tools for more frequent cleanings. A deck should be cleaned every other week during its busy season.

Patios: The same cleaning schedule applies to patios, although the cleaning methods vary. If you have a patio made with closely knit pavers, a large industrial broom such as the one recommended for decks will work well. An electric leaf blower will also suit. If your patio is a loose gathering of pavers or stones with smaller gravel between each piece, cleaning will need to be more delicate. Dedicate a household-grade broom for your patio to sweep excess fill gravel from patio paver or stones.

For spider webs and other animal homes, try to leave as much as you can intact. If necessary, you can clear door entries and windows while leaving other webs and nests in higher or lower places intact. For a natural repellant that will not harm spiders and other small insects but encourage them to relocate elsewhere, find hybrid plants at your local nursery. Different plants are bred to include the scents of herbs, such as basil, that naturally repel spiders. It's important to support spiders especially because they help keep the outdoors clean and free from bothersome insects like mosquitoes. Depending on where you live, bats will also show up in the outdoor space around your home. If you prefer them to live in another area, invest in an inviting cedar bat house they can migrate to. Believe it or not, bats are wonderful animals that help keep the number of insects down making your outdoor spaces more enjoyable.

I imagine that when you picked up this book you didn't expect to read a section praising the cleaning abilities of spiders and bats. Insights like that are exactly why this book was written. There are so many areas in your home and each requires its own set of rules for cleaning. Tools and techniques often cross over from room to room. Oftentimes, there are specific insights that won't come up in just any old search engine. This chapter captured all the small spaces that weave themselves throughout larger living areas. With plenty of technique crossover and handy tips for specific pressure points, you're ready to get these areas clean and primed for repeated use.

Chapter 11: 7 Day Cleaning Plan

Day 1: Remove Surface Clutter

Depending on the state of your home, there is going to be a lot of clutter taking up space on surfaces all over the house. That's okay. This week is about slowly breaking up that clutter and the dirt that lurks within so cleaning becomes easier and quicker. Like each day during this cleaning week, start one load of laundry and move it to the dryer. The load can be started right at the beginning of the hour and then moved to the dryer at the end.

With this day's hour, tackle the surfaces throughout your home. For convenience, you may want to use a small trash can to carry from room to room.

Bathroom

Countertop:
1. Remove any trash from the countertop or sink vanity
2. Corral products into one place on the countertop, opening up space around them
3. Alternatively, return products to their proper home on shelves or inside a medicine or storage cabinet

Shelves:
1. Remove any trash
2. Bring products together in one place on the shelf, opening up space around them

Floor:
- Pick up any clothes or trash that may have fallen

Kitchen

Counters:
1. Return food to the pantry or other storage space
2. Move dirty dishes to the sink
3. Return tools to their storage space

Shelves:
1. If your kitchen has exposed shelves for storage, remove everything that does not normally live there and move it to its proper storage space
2. Organize shelf contents to be together on one end of the shelf

Floor:
1. Pick up any food wrappers or other trash
2. Return footstools or other kitchen and cleaning tools to their proper storage space

Bedroom

Furniture tops:
1. Remove any clothing that can be worn again before washing and put in a hamper or designated spot.
2. Group together any accessories that normally stay on surface tops. For bedside tables, groupings include lamps and alarm clocks. For dresser tops, this may include watch and cases for eyewear.

Bed:
1. Remove any clothes, books and magazines. Store clothes in hamper. Stack books and magazines neatly on a side table.
2. Make your bed if it isn't already made

Floor:
1. Pick up any clutter from the floor
2. Return items to their homes if they're close by
3. If not, stack them neatly on a dresser, nightstand, or other furniture surface

Living Area

Furniture tops:
1. Remove any trash
2. Organize clutter into groups. Stack books, magazines, and mail together

Shelves:
- Remove any items that do not belong. If their home is close by, return them. Otherwise, stack them neatly on shelves to open up the space around them.

Floor:
1. Pick up shoes, blankets, or any other clutter. Stack them neatly in groups.
2. Fold blankets together on the couch.
3. Move shoes together in a row by the wall or returned to them to their mudroom racks

Other Areas:

These areas include the entryway, mudroom, closets and laundry room. Surface tops may include furniture, machines, display shelves and storage racks

1. Remove any trash from surface tops
2. In the entryway or mudroom, store keys and other items in their proper place or group them together in a basket
3. In the laundry room, return all detergents and laundry supplies to their proper place getting rid of empty containers
4. In the closet, take any dirty clothing to the hamper to be washed and return any clean clothing to hangers or drawers
5. In all areas, organize the remaining items in a group to open up space around them

Floor:

1. Move shoes, coats, books, and any other clutter to surface tops either in the space or the proper storage area for the items
2. Stack shoes in the entryway shoe organizer or the floor
3. Place any books back onto shelves in the living area
4. Hang coats found on chairs in the entryway or closet
5. Pick up any loose socks or other clothing in the laundry room and sort to be washed or put away
6. Shake out rugs in the entryway or mudroom
7. Pick up any clothing or shoes on closet floors and put them where they belong. Move shoes to their organizer. Place clothes in a hamper or hang up.

The key on this day is to touch almost every surface in your home in one hour working from the top to the bottom. Grouping items together to take up less space is intentional. You're setting yourself up for the next step in cleaning without tearing apart shelves and surface tops. At the end of the hour, you may not end up with all the shoes in the home delivered to the shoe rack, but you will have stacked all your shoes in neat groupings. This provides a positive aesthetic versus the chaos of shoes scattered around a room. The mental boost from seeing something like a clean line of shoes will encourage you to continue your progress the next day.

Day 2: Kitchen and Bathrooms Surfaces

The next step can be a little time consuming so it is conveniently broken up into two days. On this day, you're going to wipe down or dust surfaces in both the kitchen and the bathroom. The work you did to declutter the day before has prepared you for this. Items have been grouped together on surface tops so you can immediately clean an area, move the items, and clean the other parts. With no clutter to trip over, you can go directly to dusting cabinet fronts without a second thought. At the start of this hour, put one load of laundry in the washer moving it to the dryer at the end of the hour.

Gather supplies:

- 10 soft cloths (enough for one kitchen and one bathroom cleaning)
- Scrub brush dedicated to kitchen use
- All-purpose cleaner that can handle grease
- All-purpose cleaner that can disinfect
- Scrub brush dedicated to bathroom use

Kitchen: Upper Cabinets and Shelves

There will be time for a deep clean of both the upper and lower cabinets, but in this hour, we're going to focus on the areas that receive a lot of use. Identify the upper cabinets and shelves that receive the bulk of the use in the kitchen. It may just be the range hood and the refrigerator (face and handles). It could also include the cabinet where everyday dishes are stored.

- Wipe them down with a soft cloth dampened with your favorite all-purpose cleaner that can tackle grease. You can also use a homemade vinegar recipe from the recipes chapter of this book.

Countertops:

Take the same cloth used for the upper cabinets and shelves and wipe down all of the counters.

1. Begin with a small open section where you can wipe front to back without encountering small appliances or other items stored on the counter.
2. Once this section is wiped of large debris with the same soft cloth, set it aside. You'll use it again in a minute
3. Get out a fresh soft cloth and your favorite countertop cleaner that can also disinfect.

4. Spray and wipe down the section of counter
5. To speed dry, you can use a third soft cloth to wipe down the counter
6. Move countertop items to the clean section of the counter to create a new pocket of countertop to clean
7. Start the process over. With the soft cloth used to wipe down upper cabinets and shelves, wipe off large debris from a section of the clear countertop
8. Set aside and grab your soft cloth and disinfectant cleaner
9. Use the third cloth for speed drying. Return the countertop items to where they were and move on to the next section.
10. Repeat this process until you've reached all of the countertops

Lower Cabinets and Shelves:

With a fresh soft cloth (we're up to 4 so far, more if you changed cloths during tasks as they dirty), grab your favorite all-purpose cleaner with degreaser to focus on high-use areas of cabinet fronts and shelves.

1. Examine the cabinet fronts below the sink, on both sides of the range, and near the garbage can.
2. After identifying the areas, clean them one by one changing out the cloth if it gets dirty

Sink:

If there are still dishes in your sink and you can't load them into the dishwasher or dish rack because they are also full, rinse them quickly and stack on the counter next to the sink. They will be a breeze to wash or load into the dishwasher when this hour is over. By putting them back in the sink after cleaning it, you'll be motivated to get them washed so you can enjoy the fruit of your labor.

After clearing the sink of dishes, grab a soft cloth and the all-purpose cleaner that can disinfect.

1. Start with the faucet and fixtures by spraying them, wiping them down and rinsing them with a second soft cloth that's been dampened and polishing dry with a third cloth
2. With the second soft cloth sprayed with all-purpose cleaner, wipe down the area between the backsplash and the edge of the sink, working your way around the base of the faucet and fixtures
3. Using your favorite sink cleaner, which could be the all-purpose cleaner that disinfects, spray down the sink. Using a plastic bristle brush or other appropriate tool to protect the surface of the sink, scrub in a circular motion getting the cleaner in every spot.
4. Rinse the sink with water. Replace any rinsed dishes and wipe down the part of the counter where they sat while you were cleaning the sink.

Bathroom:

In the bathroom, it's imperative to disinfect almost every surface. This can be done in a 7-day clean with a little strategy. Unlike the kitchen where you're working in a circular motion around the room in addition to focusing on specific areas, the bathroom requires attention only on one area at a time.

Vanity:

To speed up the process, take any products you had grouped together during the declutter day and move them to either the floor of the shower or a space in your bedroom. The top of a dresser or shelf with just enough space to hold everything works fine.

1. With a soft cloth and an all-purpose cleaner with disinfectant, spray down the mirror of the vanity avoiding streaks from too much cleaner sprayed at once.
2. Using the same soft cloth, begin wiping down the faucet, sink, and vanity top. Using the disinfectant all-purpose cleaner, focus on spots like dried toothpaste, water spots, and similar. Try to wipe up all of these leftover products in this soft cloth.

3. Put aside the soft cloth for laundering and grab a new one.
4. Spray faucet, sink, and vanity top once more with cleaner and wipe down with the new soft cloth.
5. Continuing downward, wipe down the front and side of the vanity. Include the base that meets the floor if you have a pedestal sink.
6. Return products to the vanity top

Shower:

Remove all products placing them in the bathroom sink, or if they're dry, on a surface nearby like a shelf or similar.

1. Spray down the shower walls with your favorite shower cleaner.
2. Using a scrub brush safe for your shower wall material, scrub in large circular motions working your way from one end of the shower to the other.
3. Spray the shower area once more.
4. Using a large soft cloth, wipe down the shower starting at one end and working your way around to the other.
5. Make sure you wipe down the showerhead and handle.
6. In the shower basin or tub, spray liberally with the shower cleaner.
7. Repeat the process of scrubbing in large circular motions before wiping down with a cloth.
8. Return products to their space in the shower area.

Toilet:

With a fresh soft cloth and disinfectant cleaner, spray and wipe the cover of the toilet tank before moving down to wiping the tank itself, including the lever.

1. Grab a new soft cloth and spray with cleaner before siping down the toilet seat cover, both sides of the toilet seat, and the top of the bowl itself.
2. Use the same disinfectant cleaner in the bowl itself or use your favorite toilet bowl cleaner to clean the toilet bowl.

3. With a new soft cloth, spray and wipe down the outside of the toilet bowl making sure you wipe the base

If you have more than one bathroom in your home, begin with the one that gets used most. After completing the kitchen and the first bathroom, there is often time in this hour to tackle a powder bathroom or a second full bathroom guests use. The key is to follow the steps in the order they're laid out, beginning with gathering the right supplies before beginning.

Day 3: Bedroom and Living Areas

With the exception of the laundry room, these spaces are dry meaning dusting will be at the top of the list in each one. In this hour, you'll be cleaning around the neat piles of items organized on Day 1 giving each surface the extra sparkle that comes from a good wipe down. The order of the rooms is important. Start with the bedroom and move on to the next largest living area, like your living room. Getting these large spaces out of the way allows you to sail through the rest of the smaller spaces wrapping up in the hour timeframe. Like with the other days, put a load of laundry in the washer at the start of the hour and move it to the dryer at the end of the hour.

Gather supplies:

- 8-10 soft cloths
- All-purpose cleaner safe for furniture surfaces
- All-purpose cleaner with disinfectant

Bedroom:

To speed up the process, leave your dry duster at home for the bedroom. Grab a soft cloth and spritz a little of your favorite all-purpose cleaner safe for furniture surfaces on it before getting started.

Wipe down furniture surfaces starting with the highest points, changing out cloths as they get dirty:

1. Top of the headboard
2. Tall dresser
3. Mirror
4. Lower dresser
5. Nightstand

Wipe down the mirror front with a fresh soft cloth and all-purpose cleaner. If you notice any dust buildup on the sides of furniture, go ahead and grab a fresh soft cloth spritzed with cleaner and wipe them down.

Living Area:

Starting with the taller hard surfaces, wipe down using a soft cloth dampened with all-purpose cleaner safe for the living area surfaces:

1. Top of fireplace mantle
2. Tops of accessory furniture (side tables, sideboards, coffee tables)
3. Top of TV and sound equipment
4. Bases of lamps
5. Bases of other furniture

Entryway or Mudroom:

1. Start with the door and door handle.
2. Take a fresh soft cloth and spritz with all-purpose cleaner before wiping down the door, focusing on the toe kick area and the area around the door handle.

3. Wipe down any window component of the entryway door.
4. With a fresh soft cloth, wipe down any shelves or cabinet fronts in the entryway area.

Laundry Room:

1. Starting with the tops of the machines or countertops, use a soft cloth dampened with water to wipe off detergent residue and large debris.
2. With a fresh cloth, spray disinfecting all-purpose cleaner and wipe these surfaces again.
3. Wipe down shelves or cabinet fronts by moving products to one side, cleaning, and then replacing the products as you move from shelf to shelf

If you have additional living areas like a home office or craft room, use the living area section to help you tackle it in this hour.

Day 4: Kitchen and Bathroom Floors

If you weren't careful with wiping the contents of your countertops into your hands on Day 2, then you're probably itching to get to this day. It's worth waiting for when at the end of this hour, you have not only sparkling floors, but counters you already cleaned. Gather your supplies and dive into this hour on your journey to a clean home in 7 days. Remember to start with your load of laundry.

Supplies:

- Vacuum
- Dry mop system (mop, 4 or more pads)
- Appropriate cleaners for the floor types
- 2-4 soft cloths

Kitchen:

1. Pick up any mats that cannot be vacuumed and shake outside.
2. Vacuum the floor before setting vacuum in bathroom.
3. Apply your preferred floor cleaner to any spots on the floor.
4. Wipe each spot with a soft cloth to completely remove it.
5. Use the dry mop system on the floor and change pads at least halfway through cleaning. This will prevent dragging dirt across the floor.
6. Replace floor mats.

Bathroom:

1. Pick up any bath mats and put them in the hamper for laundering.
2. Vacuum the floor.
3. Identify any spots and apply cleaner to wipe them up with a soft cloth.
4. Using the dry mop system, mop the floors using one pad for the area around the toilet and a new pad for the rest of the bathroom floor.
5. Replace bath mats with freshly cleaned ones, if available. If not, start a load with the bath mats removed

Floors tend to look simple on paper. There's basically two steps to cleaning them: vacuum and then mop. You will most likely finish both of these rooms in less than an hour. This allows you to tackle other bathrooms in your home bringing them up to the same level as your bathroom of initial focus.

Day 5: Living Areas

The dry mop system really comes into play when trying to clean the floors of the living areas in a reasonable amount of time. With the kitchen and bathroom, you most likely had the same type of cleaner in both rooms because they had the same floor material. In the living areas, it's common for the flooring material to go from carpet to hardwood to vinyl. This shouldn't scare you, however. Grab your supplies and make the most of this power hour. Start your load of laundry before you start this hour.

Supplies:

- A vacuum that can work on hard floor, as well as, carpet. Otherwise, two vacuums if you have separate machines for the two floor types
- Dry mop system
- 4-6 soft cloths

All Living Areas

To make this section easy to follow, everything is in one list. Follow it for each living area and omit any that don't apply to the room you're in.

1. Vacuum the area, working around any neatly grouped items like shoes by moving them to get to where they sit
2. For carpet, go back to any stains and spray with your favorite carpet cleaner according to the directions on the label.
3. If possible, let the cleaner sit while you move onto the next room setting a timer for the appropriate time to remind you to go back and finish the process.
4. For hard flooring, find any tough spots and spray with cleaner before wiping up with a soft cloth.
5. For hard flooring, use the dry mop system and change out pads frequently as you cover large expanses of flooring.
6. Move around groupings of belongings to reach the floor underneath.

Day 6: Windows

You may have felt the windows were being neglected earlier in the week. That's because they're one of the easiest cleaning tasks. However, their volume necessitates their own hour devoted to making them sparkle. Gather your supplies and start your load of laundry.

Supplies:

- Window cleaner, homemade or store bought
- 15-20 soft cloths
- Step stool (optional)

Start on the highest floor of your home working in a clockwise pattern around the level. With your soft cloth in hand, spray down your cloth with window cleaner before wiping the window panes in a circular motion. Spraying directly onto the cloth prevents cleaner from running down onto the trim of the window. Make sure you wipe into the corners of the glass to prevent spots of dust being left behind. If you use too much cleaner, use a dry soft cloth to wipe the window again in a circular motion dissolving the excess cleaner without leaving streaks.

Move to the next floor down before beginning the process again. If you notice the window sills need attention, don't worry, they're part of the deep cleaning list tackled in the next chapter.

Day 7: Laundry and Catch All

At this point, you're probably wondering why you did so many loads of laundry this week without even bothering to put everything away. You may have maxed out the number of containers you have to hold clean laundry and started living out of them for clothes needed for the day. Don't worry. There's a method here. In these loads of laundry, you should have cleaned your bath mats, bed sheets, clothes, and even towels. You might be using an old sheet set on your bed you don't really like and there's a hand towel acting as a mat in the bathroom, but the point is all your favorite linens are now clean. During this hour, put them all away. Lay out the bathmats on the still fresh floor you mopped on Day 4. Put your favorite sheets on your bed. Set up a folding command post on your bed where you can lovingly fold your clothes before putting them away.

This hour is also for catching up. You can take a few minutes to get all the shoes left in the living room or catch up on dishes in the sink. Use the time to suit you.

At the end of these 7 days, you'll be amazed at what you can accomplish when you take an hour out of each day to improve your home. This challenge isn't mean to take place everyday and indeed it can't. You have commitments in other areas of your life that require your time. The purpose of this challenge is to get your home to the point where it's easy to maintain. This base level of clean saves the frustration that comes with trying to just get started in a messy home. Now that you've completed the challenge, you don't have to worry about starting to clean the bathroom only to get distracted and unmotivated by the clutter. You're now set up for seamless cleaning time that is not wasted. By allotting hours this week for focused cleaning, you're giving your future self more time to do what you please.

Chapter 12: Maintenance & Monthly Habits

After completing the 7-day cleaning challenge, you should feel one step ahead in the care and maintenance of your home. It's not easy to dedicate an hour each day for 7 consecutive days to something like cleaning. There is work to be done, errands to be run, children and pets to care for. They all take your attention and cleaning falls to the bottom of the list. One of the greatest benefits of the challenge is that at the end, you're ready to go into full maintenance mode. It's a state of being that is less intense, requires less time, and is the glue that will keep your house together. Grab a coffee or tea and your calendar and let's begin putting together your maintenance schedule.

Follow the yearly calendar: With your calendar in hand, look over your commitments during the week, month, and course of the year.

It's impossible to predict every commitment in a 12-month span, but you can determine what times of the year are the busiest. December may be far off in the calendar at this moment, but you know there's at least one holiday party, a holiday craft bazaar, and other traditional gatherings. Knowing this, don't put anything on the deep cleaning list in December. You most likely won't get to it and feel defeated when January 1 rolls around with the task unfinished.

Follow the weather: If you live in a fair weather climate where each season offers ample opportunity to be outside, you can rely less on weather patterns and more on your own schedule. If you live in a climate with distinct seasons, including one that makes it impossible to complete work outside, you'll need to balance the weather's schedule with your own. Rather than starting with the fair weather seasons, take the coldest seasons and put together everything you can do during that time. This will keep you from feeling like the warmer months are overwhelmed with cleaning tasks.

Follow your average week: Look at a recent week in your schedule that was unusually busy. You may have had a different commitment every evening or more errands than usual to prep for a big trip. If so, then look at a week where things were slow. It may have been a week where you tried tackling cleaning the entire house on a Saturday because there was finally an open weekend on your calendar. Or maybe there were multiple nights where you were home by 6pm and got to veg out in front of the TV. Now, calculate the amount of time you dedicated to cleaning in each of those two weeks. Did you clean your bathroom and get your kitchen sparkling during the slow week? Was vacuuming the living area all you managed during the busy week? Take that amount of time and divide it by 7. That's your base amount of cleaning time for each day. Since you're looking to transform your home into better shape, add 10 minutes to that daily base of time. From there, decide where in your day that time fits best. If you're a morning person, you might want to take care of cleaning tasks before you start your day. If you get a second wind after dinner, section off that time and dedicate it to checking off the tasks on you list.

Now that you've figured out exactly how much time you can devote to your home each week, you must now decide what to do with it. Using the timed methods in previous chapters for each room, begin building your weekly time allotment with these tasks. Make sure you build in some time to catch up when weeks get busier than others.

For an example of a weekly cleaning schedule with monthly habits rolled in, I have provided the schedule for my own home. I live in a climate with four distinct seasons and have been able to carve out 20 minutes a day for housecleaning.

Weekly Schedule (Year-Round):

Monday:

- Start a load of laundry and move to dryer
- Kitchen: Wipe down counters
- Kitchen: Sweep

Tuesday:

- Fold laundry from Monday
- Bathroom: Wipe down vanity and sink
- Bathroom: Clean toilet
- Bathroom: Sweep
- Bathroom: Spray vinegar cleaner in shower to squeegee off after showering

Wednesday:

- Start a load of laundry and move to dryer
- Living areas: Dust and declutter
- Living areas: Vacuum

Thursday:

- Fold laundry from Wednesday
- Entryway/laundry room: Declutter and dust
- Entryway/laundry room: Vacuum

Friday:

- Start a load of bed sheets and move to dryer
- Bedroom: Declutter and dust
- Bedroom: Vacuum

Saturday (1 hour instead of 20 minutes):

- Make bed with clean sheets
- Vacuum floors and dry mop

Sunday:

- Rest
- Make a family dinner and use the cooking time to wipe down small appliances in the kitchen, reorganize the fridge and pantry for the week

I make small changes to my weekly schedule to accommodate for more or less mess in certain areas, but I try to keep the rooms the same each day. This helps to know exactly which room is touched on which day and saves me from wondering when a certain room is going to get some attention. Some days I have more than 20 minutes. I use that time for cleaning, but I don't try to hold myself to half an hour everyday when 20 will do a good enough job. This book is to help acquire the habit of cleaning without turning you into someone who spends all their free time with a scrub brush in hand.

Monthly Cleaning

January:

- Refrigerator and Freezer: After the holidays, the leftovers begin to hoard space in the fridge. Even if you don't get around to cleaning the refrigerator monthly, make sure January is a month that gets this task done.
- Indoor Plants: This is a bonus task for homes like mine that have many plants. It's a time I take to set old newspapers over a large swath of floor in my living room to revive each potted plant. I either re-pot it or mix in new, nutrient rich soil. When it's warmer outside, all my attention goes to my outdoor plants. The winter weather gives me the excuse to dote on the house plants that bring me joy and clean air.
- Holiday storage: Many people get excited about the holidays and the decorations that come with. The joy is multiplied 10x over from the work you can do in January when putting decorations

away. During this process, inspect decorations for any breaks or deficiencies before storing. Invest in sturdy storage bins that last and take time to properly label each bin. Once complete, everything is safe and easy to find when it's time to decorate again.

February:

- Oven: After holiday baking, give your oven a good cleaning with either your favorite oven cleaner or set the self-cleaning function.
- Baseboards: Take time to wipe down baseboards in all the rooms using soft cloths and an all-purpose cleaner safe for painted or sealed surfaces.
- Replace the home air filter.

March:

- Light fixtures: Take your time cleaning each component including the lamp shade, base, and even the cord. Start at the top of your house and work your way down.
- Clean appliances: Run the cleaning cycle on your washer and clean out the dryer ducts of lint. Clean vacuums and their filters. Run a cleaning cycle on your dishwasher.

April:

- Clothes closets: When I'm already swapping out my wardrobe with the impending season change from cold to warm, I like to take all of my clothes out of the closet and dresser. I inspect each piece for defects and assess if I want to continue holding onto it. I donate what I don't keep and my closet looks fresh from decreasing the stock.
- Clean refrigerator and freezer: Make room for all the new produce showing up at your local farmer's market by repeating this task from January. Remove all food, wipe interior, wash shelves, and replace everything.

May:

- Windows: Wash the interior of all the windows in your home. Then, at the same time or a later date, clean the sills of all the built-up dirt, dead bugs, and dust.
- Outdoor Living: Set up the outdoor living area for warmer weather by bringing furniture and cushions out of storage. Sweep the area and wipe down furniture to clear the dust.

June:

- Replace the home air filter
- Window treatments: Launder or dust off window treatments throughout your home.
- Bedding: On a hot sunny day, lay out pillows and bedding like down comforters to naturally deodorize them and kill dust mites.

July:

- Baseboards: Give them a quick clean using your vacuum and the brush attachment
- Upholstery: Look over upholstered furniture for any spots and treat them with a fabric cleaner. Launder, if necessary.

August:

- Refrigerator and freezer: Before you even see holiday decorations in stores, clean out your fridge and freezer so they're ready for the holidays ahead.

September:

- Windows: Clean the interior of your windows one more time before cooler weather arrives.
- Windows: Take time and wash the exterior of all your windows to keep them sparkling through the colder months.

October:

- Garage: Take advantage of cooler temperatures to get some heavy-lifting done in the garage. Get rid of unused equipment, reorganize the storage, and sweep out the floor before putting everything back.
- Replace the home air filter

November:

- Declutter: Spend 20 minutes in each room of the house decluttering. Take unused items to be donated or consigned. Put back everything you're keeping in an organized manner. Return items that belong in other rooms in your home. This will get you ready for holiday decorating and gatherings.
- Clean appliances: Run another cleaning cycle on appliances like washers and dishwashers. Clean out the dryer duct of excess lint. Clean your vacuum.

December:

- Don't schedule any deep cleans this month if you have a lot of seasonal events.

Considering what's possible to accomplish each month of the year, you've got this. You can make a schedule that not only maintains a clean home, but keeps stress and worry away. I included the weekly cleaning list with the year-long monthly tasks because they're interlocked in their mission to keep your home spotless. They work together to avoid instances where you're spending your entire Saturday deep cleaning every part of the house because you can't remember the last time you did. With a monthly and weekly schedule, you can feel confident that every inch of your home is covered over the course of a year.

You'll notice December is blocked off from deep cleaning tasks to give yourself time for the holiday season. If December isn't that busy of a month for you, move that deep clean-free time somewhere else. Maybe you need a break in January or the middle of summer because that's when your family travels. Determine when that is and schedule it in. Give yourself a break at some point in the year to avoid burnout. It's so easy to let something as simple as cleaning get in the way of happiness and contentment. Get ahead of it and don't let it steal any more attention than it needs.

This schedule you're building for yourself will take from the rest of this book. The timed tasks and methods for cleaning each area will come together piece by piece. You'll build it according to the time you have to devote to each task. You'll also have various factors that impact how your schedule is made. If you have a robotic vacuum, your cleaning time will be devoted to preparing the area for it to run. If you have a monthly cleaning service that can help with larger deep clean projects, you'll spend less of your Saturday wiping windows or the like.

The monthly schedule is especially helpful for vacation rentals. It's not always easy to plan when a deep clean project can get done. However, if you know that in a certain month certain tasks should be completed, you can work them into your schedule around check-ins and check-outs.

To help build your weekly schedule, I've included a chart of tasks and the time they take. Gathering all the information from other chapters and adding it here will help you get started on building a schedule. You can always refer to the other chapters for more cleaning techniques and product suggestions. The following chart is your quick reference when you need it.

	<u>10 minute tasks</u>	<u>20 minute tasks</u>	<u>30 minute tasks</u>
Kitchen	• Declutter counters • Wipe down appliances	• Unload and load the dishwasher and/or dishrack • Sweep and mop floors	• Clear the counters • Clean inside appliances
Bathroom	• Clear surfaces • Wipe down surfaces	• Sweep and mop floors • Focus on sinks and toilets	• Dust surfaces like towel bars and shelves • Grout cleaning (up to 45 minutes)
Bedroom	• Make bed • Fold laundry	• Vacuum floors • Clear clutter	• Wipe down surfaces • Return items that belong in other rooms

	10 minute tasks	20 minute tasks	30 minute tasks
Living Area	• Clear surfaces • Dust surfaces	• Sweep or vacuum floors • Dry mop floors	• Return items that belong in other rooms • Wipe down furniture and spot clean upholstery
Other Areas	• Clear surfaces • Dust surfaces	• Sweep or vacuum floors • Dry mop floors	• Return items that belong in other rooms • Wipe down surfaces like doors in entryways, machines in laundry room, etc.

Most people are surprised by the amount of time they spend on cleaning each week, trying to make their house look a certain way. However, the time spent does not create the desired result. By taking that time and adding a little bit more where needed, you can work smarter, not harder to have a sparkling home. Once you've completed the 7-day cleaning challenge, the next task is implementing your new schedule. The first week will tell you everything you need to know about adjustments and improvements. Refer back to this chapter as you hone your schedule and find everything you need to boost your success.

Conclusion

You've reached the end of this book but the beginning of a new era in your home. Depending on your reading style you might have read the book cover to cover over the course of a few days. Alternatively, you might have read up to the 7-day cleaning challenge, started that, and came back to finish the rest. However you consumed this book, I hope it has changed how you see cleaning in your home. At the start of this book, you might not have known the wonders of a dry mop system and your clutter was taking over your life, as well as any free time you had on Saturdays.

Cleaning was not just a chore for you, but something you dreaded. An inescapable fact of life that you swore was out to get you. You might have tried to get your act together and find a cleaning system to work for you. This could be your first or 50th attempt at incorporating a solid cleaning game plan into your schedule. You picked up this book and with another deep breath, dove in. You took the first steps on a new journey and the pages within showed you the rest of the way. I promised you a fresh start and with each chapter, showed you the way.

Starting with tried and tested cleaning recipes, this book brought to you a new depth of knowledge when it comes to cleaning your home. There are many uses for everyday products sitting in cabinets and pantries. With the right combination, you can find the product needed to tackle any cleaning job in your home. Sometimes the mess has gotten out of hand. You inherited a dingy bathroom when moving into your new apartment or the space you want to become a vacation rental looks more like a vacation nightmare. To restore your space to a spotless clean you can maintain were lists of products to get the job done right.

As with the cleaning recipes and favorite tools, each room was scrutinized for the best way to deep clean and then maintain. The focus on deep cleaning techniques paired with their maintenance cousins was to battle every roadblock that's ever stopped you from cleaning before.

Whether it was being overwhelmed by the scope of the cleaning needed, or life getting in the way of a cleaning schedule you made. Your motivation wanes. Your space descends further into chaos with your attempts to restore your home to clean thrown in.

By sharing deep cleaning methods marked with the time they take to complete, this book empowers you to tackle everything in your home. To show you that's possible, the 7-day cleaning challenge brought you together with method of cleaning to bring your home into balance. By comparing your home at the beginning of the challenge and the end, you see firsthand what you're capable of accomplishing. Any previous attempts at maintaining a clean home wash away from memory. You're in the here and now.

A cleaning challenge wasn't enough, however. You needed to find a way to clean your home in the time already available to you during the week. You needed to work smarter and not harder in the time you were already giving to your home. By sitting down and assessing how much time that is, you were able to take the tasks and times given for each room and make a cleaning schedule that works for you.

You've found the motivation to not only clean, but to open up your space to support the life you want to live. The vacation rental you've been wanting to get started is in sight now. The dream of hosting friends and family more regularly looks like a reality. In each room, the motivation builds as you arm yourself with new techniques and tricks to keep clutter at bay and the space cleaner for longer.

In each room, you now have the tools and products needed to keep the space clean. Your focus is no longer scattered, but set precisely on different tasks based on the time they take. As you refer back to this book again and again, you'll find more of it sticking with you. As it sets in your mind, cleaning will become not only a task to be completed but an accomplishment you look forward to reaching. You'll love the way it feels to know exactly what needs to be done in each room and when.

Living rooms can be lived in and still look chic for a gathering of friends. Kitchens are always ready for cooking because of a few minutes spent strategically decluttering. Bathrooms are prepared for guests at any moment saving you any embarrassment. Entryways and mudrooms can not only take the clutter of shoes and coats, but look good doing it. Questions about "Does this need to be cleaned?" have been answered and guided steps given to achieve that clean.

Rather than spend hours on a Saturday or try to meet some arbitrary daily goal of cleaning, you sat down with your schedule and found space that already existed. You transformed the time you already spent on cleaning into time that's efficient. The time dedicated to cleaning in your schedule is satisfying because you see the end in sight. You know that when you spend an hour on a space, you're going to accomplish x, y, and z.

Instead of bouncing around to different deep cleaning tasks done in times of panic and crisis, you're already plotting out the future. You've learned to take the seasons of your life throughout the year and maximize your time with different deep cleans in different months. No more smoking ovens at the holidays because you forgot the last time you cleaned the oven. No more stuffy house in winter because it's too cold to be outside. You know exactly what needs to be done and when.

The other key points to keep in mind include:

- Look in your cabinets. Use household supplies you already have to make cleaning products.
- Find your starting point. In every room, no matter the task, there's a starting point to help you get off on the right foot and finish the tasks at hand. Whether it's working clockwise around the room, starting at the top and working your way down, or sometimes a combination of both.

- Find the right tools. From surface to surface, room to room, make sure you're arming yourself with the tools to make each cleaning task go smoothly.
- Both deep cleaning and maintenance cleaning work together to help make your home sparkle.
- Take the 7-day challenge. By dedicating an hour each day to cleaning, you can take your home from overwhelming to being ready for anything.
- Revamp your time spent on housecleaning with a schedule that combines deep cleaning tasks with maintenance ones.

All of the knowledge put forth in this book comes from years of research and lived experience. I wanted to feel in power within my home and I wanted to feel in charge when it came time to open a vacation rental. I spent countless hours and dollars trying new cleaning products and honing my must-have list to tackle anything my house threw at me. I knew long ago I didn't want to keep it all with me. I wanted to share it with others and empower them to take control of their spaces.

You have that knowledge now and thus the power to take control of your space. If there's one thing I want you to take away from this book, it's that statement. You are empowered with knowledge that can overcome any anxiety you had around cleaning. There may have been a million attempts on your part to find a cleaning solution that stuck, but this book is the last one for you. It's here to help you in every step of your cleaning journey and stay with you like a favorite cookbook. It's a reference for everything going forward and a reminder of what you can do no matter your space. Use it well and find the balance of clean that makes you feel at home.

Bibliography

Saxbe, D. E., & Repetti, R. (2009). No Place Like Home: Home Tours Correlate With Daily Patterns of Mood and Cortisol. *Personality and Social Psychology Bulletin, 36*(1), 71–81.
https://doi.org/10.1177/0146167209352864

Florida State University. (2015, October 1). Chore or stress reliever: Study suggests that washing dishes decreases stress. *ScienceDaily*. Retrieved December 11, 2019 from www.sciencedaily.com/releases/2015/10/151001165852.htm

CPSIA information can be obtained
at www.ICGtesting.com
Printed in the USA
LVHW080452280820
664417LV00016B/839